# TUGS IN THE FOG

**Joan Margarit** was born in 1938 in Sanaüja, La Segarra region, in Catalonia. He is an architect, and from 1968 until his retirement was also Professor of Structural Calculations at Barcelona's Technical School of Architecture. He first published poetry in Spanish, in 1963 and 1965, but after a silence of ten years switched to writing and publishing in Catalan. From 1980 he began to establish his reputation as a leading Catalan poet. As well as publishing many collections in Catalan, he has translated most of his own books into Spanish. *Tugs in the Fog: Selected Poems* (Bloodaxe Books, 2006) is the first translation into English of his Catalan poetry.

# Joan Margarit
# TUGS IN THE FOG
## SELECTED POEMS

TRANSLATED BY
ANNA CROWE

BLOODAXE BOOKS

ISBN: 1 85224 751 7

First published 2006 by
Bloodaxe Books Ltd,
Highgreen,
Tarset,
Northumberland NE48 1RP.

www.bloodaxebooks.com
For further information about Bloodaxe titles
please visit our website or write to
the above address for a catalogue.

Bloodaxe Books Ltd acknowledges
the financial assistance of
Arts Council England, North East.

ACKNOWLEDGMENTS
Thanks are due to Institut Ramon Llull, Barcelona,
for providing a translation grant for this book.
Thanks are also due to Joan Margarit's Catalan
publisher, Enciclopèdia Catalana, SA, for permission
to publish Anna Crowe's translations of his poems.

Cover design: Neil Astley & Pamela Robertson-Pearce.

Cover printing: J. Thomson Colour Printers Ltd, Glasgow.

Printed in Great Britain by
Bell & Bain Limited, Glasgow, Scotland.

# CONTENTS

## from STRUCTURAL CALCULATIONS (2005)

# PROLOGUE

My relationship with poetry began as I was leaving adolescence, on that beautiful island, sparsely populated and with no tourism, that was Tenerife in the fifties. Some years later, when I was going to study architecture in Barcelona, I did these journeys by sea, sometimes on those white vessels of the regular shipping-line that took four or five days, or when possible, on some cargo-ship. This would take ten days. It was on those crossings that I began to write.

Now old age has entered my life, and therefore my poetry, with the loss of the sense of the future, which has been replaced by that of a strict present. Old age is, above all, this present without a future that is made up of loss, solitude and a comfortable disinterest in what claims to be new or exotic, going back to Diderot's maxim: 'Mediocrity is characterised by a taste for the extraordinary.'

It seems to me that this kind of disinterest is a positive feeling which protects the mind against imposture, and I feel it now as the common sense of poetry, or at least of the kind that interests me, which is the strictly personal, I would say almost secret, ordering of one's own suffering, of what we are when we are alone.

Today I am glad to see these poems in the language of three of the poetic voices I love best: Thomas Hardy, Philip Larkin and Elizabeth Bishop. It all began in the setting of the StAnza poetry festival in St Andrews. I went to give a reading there where I read my poems in Catalan, with Anna Crowe, who had translated them in advance, reading them in English. When the event was over, Neil Astley, editor of Bloodaxe Books, who was in the audience, came up to me and offered to make this book. I was agreeably surprised because I was not used to editors attending poetry readings in search of possible writers to add to their list. At this point I would like to thank Neil, as well as Anna, who has translated the book. Working with her has always been an enriching experience for me.

It seems to me that these poems correspond to what have been, and are still, my own concerns, since the most important source of my poetry is subjectivity. The pure product of speculation holds no interest whatsoever for me, since I believe that poetry is not a question of content but of intensity. This is why I try to have my poems fulfil what the architect Coderch, who was my teacher (I am and have always worked as an architect), told me a house should be: 'Neither independent, nor made in vain, nor original, nor sumptuous.'

I am a Catalan poet, but these poems are also the fruits of bi-lingualism. It is not true to say that they are Catalan poems translated into Castilian, rather that they were written *almost* at one and the same time in both languages. This is the result of linguistic circumstances affecting many people who, like me, were born into a Catalan family during or at the end of the Spanish Civil War, when the fascist dictatorship banned my language and ruled that all teaching should be in Castilian. This is why I began writing in Castilian, since I had no culture in any other language. Years later I moved over to writing in Catalan, searching for that which goes deeper in all of us than literary culture. It is possible to have one or more cultural language, but often none of these helps to find the place where the poem is. As with fairytales, it is a question of entering a vault, and you have to know the password that will open it. All these matters are superfluous when the mother tongue and cultural language are one and the same. When this is not the case, the cultural language can be a cathedral built over the vault that is the mother tongue.

Thus, I gain access to the poem in Catalan, but I immediately begin to handle the Castilian version as well. I revise it a lot and, generally, the final poem bears little resemblance to the first draft, but I make all the modifications in both Catalan and Castilian at one and the same time. And all my books have been published in both Catalan and Castilian.

As far as poetry is concerned, in spite of the fact that it is written and read through what might be called our feeling intelligence, I think that the only thing that characterises it and differentiates it from prose is concision and exactness. It is the most exact form of writing in the same way that mathematics are the most exact of the sciences: poetry has to say just what is necessary (mostly without knowing what this is) to its readers.

From this exactness comes its power to console, because poetry serves to introduce within us some change that will bring a greater order in the face of life's disorder. If this happens it means that the reader has "understood" the poem at some level, enough at least to be disposed to go on thinking about it and to go on reading it, and to do this no special gift or previous disposition is necessary.

But if poetry does not require too many previous conditions, it does not mean that writing it or reading it are innocent activities, since nothing is further from poetry than ingenuous spontaneity. To be exact, poetry is the furthest limit towards which we can go as we take part in life, and in things. Beyond poetry there begins a zone on the edge of the world, a sterile brightness or darkness, surely the place to which the mystic aspires, a territory which – I admit – awakens my mistrust, because I belong to the old school of thought that suspects mystics of being mystifiers, though sometimes in spite of themselves. Poetry struggles to be the complete opposite, it attempts to live life with as little mystification as possible without falling into terror, to live with the highest dose of truth we can bear, which is not too much, because truth, as in Greek tragedy, destroys the one who unveils it. It could also be said that the poet is a strange kind of mystic, capable of saying what he or she sees: in one way it is as though words had served, by naming things, to establish a line of defence against the terror of the world and that poetry should allow us to penetrate once more – always prudently, always guarded by words – that icy infinity that begins behind the protective barrier of language.

But I also try not to forget the function poetry has of remaining faithful to what we have felt at any given moment, that is to say, of saving our memory from the wasting effects of time. Darwin wrote that 'the desire to point to any event with a heap of stones on the highest point on the horizon denotes a passion inherent in human beings'. Each poem indicates a fact in my life, but the intention at the moment of writing it goes further. Its ultimate goal is that there should be someone somewhere who, when they read it, will realise that they too have built a heap of stones in some high place in their own life in order to point to some inner event of their own.

Because for me – drawing a parallel with music – the reader of poetry is more akin to an interpreter who plays an instrument than to those who confine themselves to listening to a concert. With the instrument of his or her own sensibility, the poetry reader interprets the score of the poem. And I always imagine, in this prologue too, that I am speaking to them, this little group of men and women who, when reading my poems, must be looking for the same thing I am looking for when reading what they have written.

JOAN MARGARIT
*Barcelona, December 2005*

# TRANSLATOR'S NOTE

This book had its beginnings, as Joan Margarit indicates in his Prologue, at StAnza, Scotland's poetry festival, in March 2005. Joan's reading and the warmth of his personality had a huge impact on the audience: here was poetry of truth and directness delivered with simple, passionate conviction, and people were visibly moved. When I first began to translate the poems, I wanted to soften them, finding their directness and honesty almost too much to bear. Joan was swift to correct this, and from then on I did my best to remain faithful to what he called 'an almost excessive brutality'. His collection, *Estació de França* – the name of the station from which the poet and his wife frequently caught the train to Paris and freedom – teems with departures and arrivals, with journeys back in time to the end and aftermath of the Spanish Civil War, and is imbued with the spectre of war and with memories, above all, of his father. Margarit's work reveals how harsh existence was then in Catalonia, the squalor and greyness of life in Barcelona under Franco, and the pain, despair and joy of love and sex.

Margarit's collection, *Joana*, was written during the final eight months of life of his beloved, handicapped daughter. Like Douglas Dunn's *Elegies*, these are poems that dare to deal with grief and loss and loneliness using the only means at a poet's disposal, words. Joan Margarit is certainly not afraid of words, and these deeply moving poems are both a continuing conversation between father and daughter, and also a shining celebration of her life. 'September beach' borrows the cry of Poe's raven, that famous *Nevermore*, to devastating effect. 'Final walk' imagines Joana herself speaking as she never could in life, leaving her illness behind 'like a sweaty skin', and with a characteristically realistic touch as she looks back at her balcony, 'the iron bars like a music-stave.' Another poem recalls Margarit's Professor of Deep Foundations in the School of Architecture, Bonaventura Bassagoda, who began every lecture with the words:

> ...Good morning, gentlemen. Today
> it is so many years, so many months and so many days
> since my daughter died.
> And he would wipe away a tear.

Joana's presence permeates Margarit's work: the happiness her company brought him he had already immortalised in the much anthologised poem from *Etchings*, 'The eyes in the rear-view mirror', which should be read alongside 'Dark night in Balmes Street', the poem which looks back to the night she was born, in order to grasp just how far and from what depths of despair her life had redeemed him.

Joan Margarit came to occupy the same chair as his old professor, and his subsequent book, *Structural calculations*, pays homage to his profession. These are poems that continue to deal with the absence of Joana. The poet is beginning to internalise and cope with her loss, but that can sometimes come to seem in itself like forgetting (as anyone who has been bereaved will know), even like an act of betrayal. In his poem, 'Safety', he writes, 'For me pain is a necessary weapon against oblivion.' 'Motorway' addresses the Chilean poet, Neruda, whose work Margarit greatly admires. Neruda and his Dutch wife had a mentally and physically handicapped daughter, but the outbreak of the Civil War allowed him, as consul, to send them back to the Netherlands, while he returned to Chile with his mistress, and so lost the possibility of permitting his life to be enriched by having to take care of his daughter: Neruda's 'love-poems...hid her from sight as the wind / might cover a dead bird with fallen leaves'. Death and old age are the common theme running through this collection, but although Margarit's poetry confronts the worst that life can throw at us, it is never merely bleak. Even the final poem, 'The dead', with its memories of his little sister dying of meningitis in the cold postwar dark, of his father's imprisonment as a former Republican soldier, and of his own daughter's death, all set within the framework of a playground game, ends on a note of clear-eyed acceptance. Like a Rembrandt drawing, it is the darkness, the shading, that inform and intensify the light, and Margarit reminds us that it is not death we have to understand, but life. His poetry draws the reader into a warm, humane embrace and, in sharing his solitude with us, makes us feel that we are not alone.

English readers will recognise in the melancholy and candour of Margarit's poetry a close affinity with the poetry of Hardy, who is one of the poets he regards most highly, and whose work he has translated into Castilian. His willingness to confront the dark side of life likewise makes him a close reader of Larkin, and there are echoes too of Elizabeth Bishop, with whom Margarit shares a fine eye for the telling, concrete detail and her liking for geographical frames. His poems are anchored in the real world, in physical circumstance, real places, specific times. Joan Margarit is a practising architect, and his poetry has a sense of being structured in space and time. The calculations of architecture are counterbalanced by strongly expressed feeling, and this tension and balance finds expression in a sense of risk that pervades much of his work: In 'First love', the clasp-knife he buys secretly when a child goes on being hidden behind books, then in a drawer among his wife's underwear, and finally, years later, letting the blade spring open, he finds it still to be '[s]ensual, cold. Nearer my neck'. In 'Safety', with its building-site imagery, he reminds us that 'the man installing the safety-net has no net', and in 'Dawn at *Cap de Creus*', the poet walks along the top of the headland, dangerously close to the edge of the cliff, and we are told that life's final journey is 'the one that runs along the edge of the abyss'.

Drawing an analogy with architecture, Joan Margarit has remarked that just as mathematics is the most exact of the sciences, so poetry is the most exact of the arts: a poem has to build the strongest structure that the fewest words are capable of supporting. While he uses metaphor sparingly, one of his greatest strengths is the sheer power of his imagery. His poem, 'Secrets' (*Structural calculations*), tells the story of one of his parents' neighbours, a pitiful prostitute with whom the young Margarit sometimes shared a coffee, and who is found dead in her bath. When the poet's family move into her flat, now newly painted, 'not a trace of her remained / except for an unpainted hole below the wash-hand basin / just where the exit-pipe went into the wall.' There is something terrible and absurd about a woman's life being reduced to this 'unpainted hole', but it can also be seen as a powerful image of our enduring need to reclaim the past. It is also true that the past, that foreign country that Hartley warns us about, can sometimes bring its own dangers, as in 'Asking' (*Structural calculations*), where the poet tells us, 'Memories now are / canisters of poison-gas abandoned / in old battle-fields full of flowers.' In 'Young partridge' (*Structural calculations*), one of his most pared-down and moving poems, the comparison between the wounded bird and his dead daughter is gently suggested at the beginning when the poet tells us, 'It was crouching in a furrow, and when I picked it up / it felt as though your hand was in mine.' The movements of the wounded bird are truthfully and exactly observed, so that the reader continues to make the comparison for herself:

> It tried to fly, but with great effort,
> trailing its wing, dragged itself along the ground
> before hiding itself behind a stone.

And the same dispassionate eye is at work in the description of the child waiting in the slaughter-house to buy blood, in 'The oracle' (*Etchings*). He places his pot in front of one of the goats who are tethered and hobbled, and the man 'with no hurry / armed with a knife, cuts its throat'. The poet tells us he has tried for years to understand the meaning of the sound of that red jet – a meaning which, as at Delphi, was 'difficult and obscure' – and concludes uncompromisingly: 'I'm doing that now, pissing blood.' 'The oracle' is just one of many poems that confront age and sickness, and where the poet chooses to place the imagery within the context of classical literature.

There are many references to the *Iliad* and the *Odyssey* and, Barcelona being where it is, it is hardly surprising that Homer's sea should be a constant and complex presence in Margarit's poetry, both as a storehouse of memory and an image of death, and we find the poet turning to it for consolation, interrogating it after the death of Joana, listening to its heartbeat rhythms, seeing how, at night, 'it shines like a horse in its stall', and sinking in it like an old, rusting cargo vessel. Joan Margarit's cultural references are wide and rich, and any reader of his poems is likely to find himself or herself in the presence of writers such as Tolstoy, Defoe, Baudelaire, Czeslaw Milosz, Poe, Hopkins, Wilde, Hemingway, Raymond Chandler, Jules Verne, or composers and musicians such as Bach, Tchaikovsky, Billie Holiday, Art Tatum and Charlie Parker, or painters and sculptors like Cézanne, Van Gogh and Miquel Blay. The city of Barcelona too – its mean and sordid backstreets of the fifties and sixties, the crowded Rambla, its dirty port and docks, the cemetery on the top of Montjuïc – lives and breathes in these poems like a character in its own right.

Catalan is an extremely rewarding language to translate into English. Its mixture of harsh and mellifluous sounds, and monosyllabic and iambic patterns of stress means that it is often possible to find close sound and rhythmic equivalents in the mix of Anglo-Saxon and Latin components in English. Translating Joan Margarit's poetry has been a challenging and immensely satisfying task. As soon as I began reading the poems he was to read at StAnza I knew that this was a great poet and that I wanted to read everything I could lay my hands on. I sensed that this spare, muscular language, the simplicity hiding a complex lyricism, would present formidable challenges to the translator: there would be no place to hide. I felt convinced, however, that this was poetry whose warmth and candour and vulnerability would be valued and understood by English readers. It pulls no linguistic tricks and yet its imagery is richly satisfying. Above all, this is poetry that tackles the deepest questions life demands us, that offers no easy answers, no palliatives to suffering, but which holds out to the reader the poet's own joy and pain and asks him or her to share it. In sharing it we emerge changed, and for the better. Translating Joan Margarit's poems, and working with him, has been a joy and a privilege.

ANNA CROWE

*from*

# THE FIRST FROSTS:

## SELECTED POEMS 1975-1995

## Poem for a frieze

It was a drawing on so fine a paper
that the wind carried it off. From the highest
window into the farthest distance, streets, the sea:
the time I'll never get back.
I have searched for it on winter beaches,
when a lost drawing is hardest to bear.
I have followed the routes of every wind.
It was the pencil drawing of a girl.
Lord, how I've searched for it.

*from* **RAINLIGHT** (1986)

## Odysseus in Ithacan waters

You are nearing the island and now you know
the meaning of life, what fate is.
Your bow will be dust upon the shelf.
Dust, the loom and its work.
The suitors who camp in the courtyard
are shadows whom Penelope dreamed.
You are nearing the island: the sea batters
the rocky shore as time does the *Odyssey*.
No one has ever woven your absence
or unravelled oblivion with never a rustle.
Moreover, for no known reason,
Penelope is sometimes a shadow of your dream.
You are nearing the island: the gulls
that cover the beach do not move
as you cross it leaving no footprint,
for you never existed: you are legend.
Maybe there was an Odysseus who died at Troy,
but in the dream of a blind poet
you go on escaping. On Homer's rigorous
and eternal brow, with every dawn,
a solitary Odysseus disembarks.

# On a beach in the Aegean

A hospital ship sails the rusty
eyes of winter, and the big rivets
in the hull are the words of a war.
Laden with military gangrenes,
its lights slowly enter the fog.
They are memory's expeditions
to the hospital ship of Rupert Brooke,
buried on a beach, on a Greek island.
Desire shines with intensity in the morning
and on the seductive skin of the waves:
the link with the future is this sand
where the bodies of tourists lie tanning,
many of them English while, out to sea,
the cold and feverish evenings return,
and, armour-plated and grey, this Charon
is passing with the lad shrouded in fog.

*from* **RED AGE** (1991)

## Love and time

Remember when you were still unaware
that life would have no mercy on you.
Love and time: time that is inside us
like the sand of a river which, little by little
changes the shape of a coast.
Love, which has replicated in your eyes
the clarity of the treasure-island.
Sensual, solitary, surrounded
by the sonorous old age of the sea,
and by the military cries of gulls.
An old man's clandestine dream.

# The treasure-island

Look at it through the window-panes. Years ago
you began moving away because you were afraid
of dropping anchor in the sensuous, shining air,
where now your memory ventures.
Look through the window: you can hear music,
and the smell of coffee is wafting
hospitably through the house. But you yearn
for the foggy splendour of the coast,
the silence of the island that has come back,
dangerous and sheer, this morning.

# Woman of spring

Behind words you are all I have.
It's sad never to have lost
a home because of love.
It's sad to die surrounded by respect and reputation.
I believe in what happens in a poem's starry night.

*from* **THE MOTIVES OF THE WOLF** (1993)


## Mother and daughter at breakfast


She is looking at you and feels how safe
you are behind your smile. She notices how you pick up
your cup of coffee slowly,
the serenity of your loose white pyjamas
as you glance through the morning paper.
Her peace is a reflection from you,
who allowed her to have her first memories
in the quiet corner of this house.
She looks at you with an adolescent's eagerness,
but she doesn't know that, if she feels safe,
it is because you don't tell her about the cupboard
you can't bring yourself to tidy,
or about the record you're afraid to hear again,
or the letters you cannot burn.
Maybe, when she comes home one night, she'll realise
where the serenity of the morning begins,
what reserves, sometimes of resignation,
and always of defeat, this peace enjoys.

## Beginnings and endings

Once, I was a girl with a future.
I could read Horace and Virgil in Latin,
recite the whole of Keats by heart.
But when I entered the grown-ups' caves,
they caught me and I started to bear
the children of a stupid, conceited man.
Now I drown my sorrows whenever I get the chance
and weep if I remember a line of Keats.
When you're young, you don't know
that you can't stay in one place forever.
And you marvel if the man or woman
you longed to place your trust in never appears.
You don't understand, when you're young, that beginnings
have nothing to do with endings.

## Sea-urchin

Under the shallow water of the coast
I anchor my suit of armour. I make no mother-of-pearl,
no pearls, beauty does not matter to me:
I am sorrow's warrior who, with black spears,
hides in a cleft in the rock.
Travelling is risky but, from time to time,
I move using my spines as crutches
and the waves tumble me in my clumsiness.
In the dangerous sea I search for the rock
I'll never have to move from. Inside my armour
I am my own prisoner: the proof
of how, without risks, life is a failure.
Outside, there is light and the song of the sea.
Within me, darkness: safety.

# Self-portrait

It was left over from the war, the old cloak
of a deserter on my bed. At night I felt
the rough touch of years that were not
the happiest of my life.
In spite of everything, the past ends up being
a brotherhood of wolves, melancholy
for a landscape skewed by time.
What remains is love – not philosophy,
which is like an opera – and, above all,
no trace of the damned poet: I am afraid,
but I get by without idealism.
Sometimes, tears slide down
behind the dark lenses of my glasses.
Life is the cloak of a deserter.

# The banquet

Her thigh-bones broken under the weight of ninety years,
suspicious and greedy, my mother-in-law watched us closely,
and that coward of a father-in-law, chronically obese,
held his tongue in ten languages. My son, with a dark,
cold hole in his head, sat stuffing himself with food,
his face in front of the television.
My brother was gorging himself to death, swelling visibly
and uttering obscenities at the white table-cloths.
My parents, withered and dumb from years of mutual hatred,
wore on their faces a look of terminal loneliness.
This was a moral banquet, disgusting, fantastical.
Having salvaged our friendship from the wreck,
you smiled as you gazed at me,
but so many years of monsters have been relentless.

## Midsummer night's dream

We have stopped the car
beside a wall of cypresses.
It's thirty years we've lived together.
I was an inexperienced youth and you
a warm and helpless girl.
The last opportunity is casting
its shadow over the moon.
I am an inexperienced old man.
And you a helpless middle-aged woman.

# First love

In the dreary Girona of my seven-year-old self,
where postwar shop-windows
wore the greyish hue of scarcity,
the knife-shop was a glitter
of light in small steel mirrors.
Pressing my forehead against the glass,
I gazed at a long, slender clasp-knife,
beautiful as a marble statue.
Since no one at home approved of weapons,
I bought it secretly and, as I walked along,
I felt the heavy weight of it, inside my pocket.
From time to time I would open it slowly,
and the blade would spring out, slim and straight,
with the convent chill that a weapon has.
Hushed presence of danger:
I hid it, the first thirty years,
behind books of poetry and, later,
inside a drawer, in amongst your knickers
and amongst your stockings.
Now, almost fifty-four,
I look at it again, lying open in my palm,
just as dangerous as when I was a child.
Sensual, cold. Nearer my neck.

# Smiling

Do as the pilots did, in little feluccas,
setting out when there was most danger,
on stormy nights: the whore comes out
made-up with moonlight, with a smile,
into the undertow of an ancient and swelling sea.
What bad weather, those Saturday nights,
and how many boats with rough sea in their eyes,
always searching for the same haven.
I pity you if, in the eyes of your love,
you have never seen the smile of a whore.
You're unfortunate if, when bad weather comes,
you do not see in the eyes of your love, making
its way with a tiny light, this felucca
that is crossing the storm for you.

# Loverman

From the basement a golden sound
reaches the dirty snow. The night is cold and sad
if it isn't fired with drugs and drink.
But the sax, with its backing of drums,
has the exact hardness of music
that vanishes with the dawn and takes its leave
like an affectionate prostitute.
Baudelaire listened to Parker's
melody in an indigo-skinned woman.
Evil is one part of beauty.
That's why Parker, in this piece,
allows the sax to wander following the shadow
of a woman who dances, her eyes closed
and in nobody's arms in the dark.

# Tugs in the fog

Shining companion of the night,
bright disc of the moon:
you travel along the beach beside me
lighting up the rooms
where the lovers are mirrors
grieving at night's ending.
You and I wander through the tumbled city.
There are sheets of newspaper dragging along
like wounded warring seagulls
that die along the jetty, and love
letters which, like old business receipts,
have settled up with my memories.
When the journey into darkness begins,
it's important to choose one's company: I have chosen
the rivers of thick, shining sounds
from two golden weapons, two trumpets:
one of them black, the warm sound Clifford makes
like a bonfire in the street in the midst of a blizzard,
and the white trumpet of Chet Baker –
which can be heard with great difficulty
in the fetid darkness near the signs of dismal hotels.
I go past walls that threaten me
and steps down to the metro encumbered by heaps
of cardboard where those asleep inside are hidden.
Shades of musicians are playing in the night.

I was hoping for an agreement on aims
and there was no aim.
I was hoping for the shipwrecked man's
old passion for lighting a fire beside the sea
and no one wanted to be rescued.
I was hoping to be able to count on people
in the matter of poetry, and values.
I didn't know that meant growing old,
that everyone was miles away, and that the future
was already made from an unknown art.
I got to know a woman: we danced
and together we listened to an *Autumn Leaves*
like this that, now, the plane trees on the Rambla

are murmuring with their leaves in the night.
She was an orderly woman, with beautiful hands:
my wife, ah God! And how she danced,
singing each song softly in my ear,
and how she laughed when I embraced her
tightly, afraid I would lose her.
Now it's the night I embrace and I listen to *Loverman*
where Charlie Parker mistakes the tempo.
The street-lights in the distance
are like the glassy eyes of a dog
that pines for someone who is absent.
The music consoles, nothing more:
when it plays it's inside me, and it has searched
for me in the worst of my sorrows,
which it interprets clearly,
without hope, but with feeling.
The city of my future has tumbled down.
I walk among legends
trampled for the autumn of the body, and I still find
fleeting flashes of welcome
like the *Cafè de L'Òpera*,
while beside the steps of the jetty,
at the end of the Rambla, between the barges,
a dead mermaid is floating,
tugged by the dirty water.

# Raymond Chandler

In each one of us there is a crime novel.
Grief stands in for crime, and love for a woman
is the novel's hard and honest detective.
To fall asleep exhausted, hearing someone crying,
to be hard up, out of work, this
is the police station where we are questioned
about nothing but loneliness.
Nobody's innocent: behind the closed door
of our eyes there is gambling until daybreak.
A failed love means going back to a poor part of town
to sleep for hours in a hotel by yourself.
Memories are finger-prints
at the scene of the crime, the false evidence
put together by bent policemen.
We are a foggy street, the setting for a thriller.

# Going to Reading

With every train comes a press of people
who hurry past him in the rain.
Standing handcuffed between two guards,
he wears the degrading prison uniform,
his hair dripping. He is a grotesque giant.
On the central platform on Clapham's
squalid station, Oscar Wilde –
who wasn't a genius – never was one so much
as when somebody spat in his face.

There is poetry written while dancing with life,
with the whore-on-the-corner life. This is the Reading road.
A road unknown to so many poets
who have never been spat in the face by anyone.

# End of the reading

I'm dazzled by the spotlights
when I gaze into the darkness where you are sitting.
The spotlights are the illusion
of shadow where you all listen to the clarity
of my blindness: we all carry
within us a dark auditorium
listening in silence to some story
of hopeless seduction.
Loving means being remote.
Love means being a stranger, but you
are the hospitality of this silence
that has listened to me knowing that inside you
I have ceased to exist, that I shall have been
no more than the much-loved shadow of someone else.

*from* **ETCHINGS** (1995)

## Don't throw away your love letters

They will not abandon you.
Time will pass, desire – this arrow
of shadow – will rub itself out
and the sensuous, intelligent, loveliest faces
will hide in a looking-glass within you.
The years will fall and books become boring to you.
You will stoop even further,
and lose even poetry.
The cold noise of the city against the window-panes
will gradually become the only music,
and the love letters that you'll have kept,
your final reading-matter.

# Background tenderness

On the old jazz records I also like
to listen to the noise coming from the audience.
There is someone calling out huskily,
happy with how the musicians are playing.
There are bursts of applause; a glass breaking.
The breathy sound of the place in the suburbs
of a southern city. A few unique moments
that return each time from the past.
Life after death must be
something like that: a lost
murmur of voices from a night with music.
And our immortal soul must be
this precise moment, fragile and brief,
when a glass rings on an old jazz record.

# Domestic affair

Alone in the house and looking through cupboards.
I find ancient road-maps,
contracts that have expired, fountain-pens
that will write no more letters, old calculators
with no batteries, watches that time has routed.
The past has made its nest in the bottom of drawers
like a sad rat. Clothes hang empty
like old characters that have been playing us.
But suddenly I come across your lingerie
the colour of night, of sand; sheer, with tiny embroidery.
Knickers, suspenders and stockings that I unfold
and which send me back to the shining but mysterious
depths of sex and love: the thing which really
gives life to a house, like the lamps and lights
of cafés and ships in an unknown port.

## The oracle

It's you as a child, carrying a jug and you're waiting
at the slaughter-house to buy blood.
On the cement floor there are some benches
where rows of goats are tethered,
with neck outstretched, hobbled and bleating.
You've placed the jug beneath one of them,
black and soft. Unhurriedly, a man,
armed with a knife, has cut its throat.
Just as at Delphi, the message
of the red jet gushing into the jug
with the same sound you're hearing now,
was difficult and obscure. You've spent
forty years trying to understand it.
You're doing that now, pissing blood.

# The eyes in the rear-view mirror

We have both grown accustomed, Joana,
for this slowness,
when you lean on your crutches, and climb out of the car,
to start off a sally of car-horns and their abstract abuse.
Your company makes me happy,
and the smile of a body so far
from what was always called beauty,
that tedious beauty, so far-off.
I have exchanged it for the seductiveness
of tenderness that lights up the gap
that reason left in your face.
And, if I look at myself in the rear-view mirror,
I see a pair of eyes I do not easily recognise,
for in them there shines the love left
by looks, and light, the shadow
of everything I have seen,
and the peace your slowness reflects back to me.
So great is their wealth
that the eyes in the rear-view mirror don't seem to be mine.

# My father's face

I look at you among the crowd and you do not see me.
The strolling musicians blend their sounds into a noisy concert.
I see on your face the burn
which the habit of looking at you had already cancelled.
Your distant history
sinks in the dark and narrow streets
in the neighbourhoods of the Rambla.
Somewhere, perhaps, there still exists the kitchen
where you fell from your mother's arms
into the burning oil.
The years with you weigh on me,
piled like snow on a tiled roof.
You haven't seen me, and my eyes, like lips,
rub your days-old stubble
and the old burn which cuts across
your face and your life.
We have all fallen from someone's arms
and the horrific scar ends up being
a mark of love that accompanies us.

# Astapovo

In the small hours, when only clocks
can be heard in the darkness,
I picture him fleeing aged eighty
on a Russian train that was going south,
the south of anywhere the old want to go.
Tolstoy feared that winter
that followed him for years
as far as the station bed that was death's,
at night while the telegraphist typed out
the shortest and cruellest of his stories.
He wanted to travel faster than the cold,
and his train remained covered forever
by the snowflakes falling through the night
in the little station of Astapovo.
I have started my flight much earlier
because I learned from him
that you have to pull into the final station
at great speed. In this way, death
has no time to signal to us
waving his lamp from the track
and, with a click, switches the points.

# The first frosts

I went with you to the museum in the park.
It was a winter morning. We stopped
in front of *The first frosts*, a sculpture
in grey marble: an old man who gazes,
naked, into the distance,
while the wind drags dry leaves along.
*Life and art are one and the same*, you said to me.
But I saw only a piece of cold
and rather rhetorical marble, and was thinking about girls.
Between that day and now, like a sea,
my life stretches out.
And crossing this grey sea my memories
come, black hulls of ships.
I have come back to the museum this morning,
and I think of you while I walk across the park
gazing into the distance and surrounded
by dead leaves that the wind drags along.

*from*

# ESTACIÓ DE FRANÇA

(1999)

# A man and a woman, a city

The train stops, wrapped
in the leaden mist that deadens
the noise of the streets, the iron hooters,
the discord of a bad music.
A taxi drops me at an impersonal centre.
It is an ugly city that waits for me
with the dullness of an aged hetaira.
But I'm beginning to retrieve a few places,
houses, pavements,
the lights of some shops, that bar.
My walk goes on restoring to me little by little
a voice in the mist and a music
with a lyric written for life.
How they change, the streets, as my memory
gradually recognises them.
There is no ugly city,
no man or woman
so wretched that they cannot be
you and me in this love story.

# Old murderers among us

Memories, closed up tightly, one inside another,
like *matrioshka* dolls, the smaller
the further away they come from.
The grown-ups' fear was in their hands
as they grasped mine: my mother's hand,
gripping my hand, is still with me,
the mute face of the man whose hair, in the space
of a few days, turned white, and that silence
which in visiting hours turned
the political detention-centre back into a school,
with a well of quicklime in the middle of the yard.

# Landscape near the airport

It still has a look of middle-class summer holidays
and at the same time of clandestine adventures,
but it's already a suburb, with the city
on the horizon, the beach running all the way.
Day is breaking, the bricklayers have lit
a bonfire with scraps of wood at the foot of a building.
Streets running between empty gardens
peter out at the beach with a fine
coating of sand covering the asphalt.
Closed-up, its paint peeling off, an old sailing-club
looks at a rusty sun rising out of the sea.
A plane flies low over it
with – on the sea's side – its fuselage
filmed over with a rosy patina.
Vulgar and full of people when summer comes,
dignified and desolate during winter,
these outskirts are just like love.

## Estació de França (1946)

You came home from the war with a tiny
military cap of khaki cloth:
right side out, a common soldier's, inside out
with officer's stripes.
You fled to France when Lister
went about shooting deserters
in the camps and villages near the frontier,
and you saved yourself pretending to be a lieutenant
in charge of demolitions during the retreat.
I was three when you came home
from the prison at Santoña.
Tenderness had deserted you:
like the whole country,
you went about turning yourself into a fascist.

You used to go to Girona to work,
on those terribly slow postwar trains.
You did simple construction-work: it was the time
when iron was scarce, you used to build
fishermen's huts, with brick walls
and tiled vaults in those little villages
that Pla used to speak about, fresh and clean
as the gleaming scales on those fish
that brimmed the boats at dawn.

Every Saturday the train used to run late
and it would be getting dark beneath the iron
and glass dome of the *Estació de França*,
with the smell of coal on the platforms
and the wet counter in the buffet.
From a long way off she and I would recognise you
among the carriages, the smoke and the crowd.

Now I am gazing at the trains and platforms
with the old eyes of that child.
Where the dome ended there is the night,
as dark as the postwar nights.
The yellowish clock above the tracks

marks the hour of death's train,
which you board with the military
cap – officer's side out – in charge
of blowing up the bridges during the retreat
from a time that will never come back to find us.

# Uncle Lluís

*These blue days and this sun of childhood.*
(Last line of poetry written by Antonio Machado at Collioure)


Buried in the mud of the Ebro, heroism.
But it was still important, even for the defeated –
already dressed in shabby civilian clothes –
to keep that dark-eyed glance,
a cheeky neighbourhood lad with his easy laugh.
Exiled, he was put on a train.
During those lengthy stops in the night,
on the wooden seat, between rifles,
he feels how war is a huge wild beast
pushing him with its claws to Bilbao,
with no kit and empty pockets.

They leave him on the platform one grey morning.
Tired by the journey and by defeat
he washes in a fountain and, deep in his eyes,
there shine his epic and the weapons
of long ago, the old weapons of those Sunday
dances in the tawdry open-air bars of Montjuïc.
He searches out the streets of tarts and hovels.
Close beside her, he smells her cheap
scent and the dark glance of eyes
where the mascara has left
black flags of dead anarchists.
Her nails, of a dirty red,
are flags that the Ebro was dragging away.
And I am proud to write again,
as in poetry's good days,
a poem about a whore
who saved herself and a man through love.
This happened when the war was over.
Meanwhile, for me the blue days
and sun of childhood were passing.

# White flowers in the mist

Grey sheets of frost
covered the almond terraces,
but the rains came like masks
and the grass erased the mirrors of cold.
The warm air in winter's eyes
began to lie to the grey wings
of wandering birds in the naked trees.
In a single mild night
with the gloom of images in the mirror
the flowers on the almond trees opened.
You too arrived at a time of cold
and loneliness: love was a breeze
over the grey frost. Forgotten flowers
wafted a scent of spring
in the frozen fields, warm snow
of ephemeral white flowers. Sadly
I recall them in that winter
that froze them in a single night.

## *García Lorca* **Express**

You come in slowly to the platform:
you are in the iron and in the strength
of the diesel engine, in the gleaming
wheels that cut through the cold.
A moon you never sang of,
the one that follows the trains,
lit up the tracks for you in the night.
All your murderers are old men by now.
Or dead like you, you who come back at dawn
in the shape of this night-train.
The shadows of the war, within me,
come from childhood's great fear.
Those armed people
could be these faces I now see
under the roof of the *Estació*
*de França*, an iron memory
of those military trains leaving at night,
with no lights, on their way to the front at Teruel.
Ancient strength of the hatred that is hidden
like the bones of the skull.
They might be these faces, these eyes.
Old city, old trains, none of it do I trust.

# Piety

The interval between two trains. He has come
searching for that war of childhood.
It is pathetic trying to converse,
at fifty, with a father aged twenty.
Beside the old muddy river of the battle,
the wind sways the weeds in front of the tombstone.
It is a youthful eternity passing
like the waters of the Ebro, far from home.
The afternoon is becoming a bell
with dark birds in the paths through the reeds.
He left him this small grey past,
cut short by some Mauser's bullet.
Suddenly he finds himself weeping
like a father at his son's grave.

# The suitcase

The clinic, going back to a time when it was a big house
with a garden in the lofty suburbs, still retains that air
of waxed parquet and big magnolia flowers.
She has registered at reception and is waiting
for someone to call her to go up to her room.
Love is many years ago, but she still
has the danger flag hoisted
on a beach where there is no one.
She thinks of the men who loved her
and whom she rejected, through cowardice
or faithfulness. One of them used to sing
*boleros* at the Rigat, and always dedicated
the most ardent songs to her with a glance.
None of them is here now. And men-friends
are already distant affairs, from when the body
was not a sordid subject of conversation.
She runs them all into one and they dance together
on a night of her youth,
when the other couples gradually stopped
leaving them alone in the middle of the dance-floor.
Being alone, that's all there is now: also that dance,
the dance-floor under the spotlights of an operating theatre
one postwar night at the Rigat.
And also, beside her feet, the old suitcase that
mechanically, while she broods on these things,
she strokes as though it were a dog.

## The girl at the traffic-lights

You are the same age that I was
when I began to dream of finding you.
I didn't yet know, just as you
haven't yet learned, that some day
love is this weapon loaded
with melancholy and loneliness
which is now aimed at you by my eyes.
You are the girl I was searching for
for so long when you didn't yet exist.
And I am that man to whom
you will one day want to walk towards.
But then I shall be far away from you,
as far as you are now from me at these traffic-lights.

# Drifting

*Estació de França:* the train remained empty.
For you and me, it was likewise the end.
In a rubbish-bin, a bouquet of roses:
somebody never came
and somebody left their hopes behind.
– We build to save the memory of something,
you said while we walked past them.
Just what another had left behind
became for me a symbol.
And I thought that what you and I were leaving –
like that bouquet of roses in the dim
light of the *Estació de França* –
would remain in who knows whose memory.
– We build so we don't get lost, you were saying.
And what we have lost is what can save us
in the unknown memory of others.

# Swimming pool

I wasn't afraid of the water, but of you,
it was your fear that made me afraid,
and the deep end where the tiles couldn't be seen.
You gripped me, I still remember
the strength of your arms forcing me
while I tried to cling on to you.
I learned to swim, but later,
and for a long time I forgot that day.
Now that you will never swim again,
I see the blue still water ahead of me.
And I understand that it was you who clung
to me in order to try to get through those days.

# The sea

Like the dark backs of a herd of colts,
the waves draw near, collapsing
with a dull but lyric murmur
that Homer was the first to know how to listen to.
Weary from their long gallop,
they begin to tremble.
Then they moan, hoarse with pleasure,
like a woman in the arms of her lover.
The waves, later, start
to hurl themselves, foaming, like wolves
that may have scented prey.
The setting sun, arriving from behind me,
lays red medals on their backs.
In the sand's wet edge
I see your footprints and, through the air,
your body's golden shadow passes.
So, it was about you, that the sea
with its deaf-mute gestures, was warning me.
It is saying that the place, within me, that you occupy
will be part of hell if you leave it empty.
That in the depths of this love there comes back to wait for me
the desolation of my twenty-year-old self.

# Architecture

Suspicious, they open the door to me, they grumble,
cursing the government, and while I look at
the beams, they lapse into self-pity.
I have entered a room where someone's asleep
after a night shift and it feels as though I'm in
the stifling hold of a cargo ship.
They will bear a great deal, they say, not talking about
the flats but themselves, while gazing at them
from portraits above the furniture is death.
People and walls are living together and cracking.
Black verdigris has rotted at one and the same
time the souls, the ceilings and terraced roofs
where the newly-retired are planting camellias.
The houses no longer seem to me to be made of stones,
or steel, or timber, or pipes.
Or proportions, colours, space,
axes of symmetry. For me
they are this tedium, like an icy wind
I feel in my face already, there on the staircase,
as though a Greek temple were rotting away.

# The German teacher

In that secondary school in the aftermath of war
I must have picked up a smattering of Greek
and left with some veneer of the classics.
But, if learning anything in that place
was hard enough, the subject with less than nothing
going for it was German, with Berlin
then in ruins, blackened under the snow.
Of our two languages, mine
was a persecuted, hers a defeated tongue.
In a tiny room in the mansion that housed
the school, as I went into class,
I'd always find her on her knees, scrubbing
beside the bin and talking to herself.
I know no German, and in general have
no good memories of any Germans,
but I have never forgotten that woman's grief.
Now that I'm taking stock of what I am
I'm on my knees feeling the cold of icy tiles
in order to wipe away the past, as she was doing
scrubbing the red border of the tiled floor.

# Farewell

In the early morning, under the glittering grubs
of the night sky, among the ploughed fields,
here at Forès where, transparent and cold,
the winter night wipes the panes clean with wind,
to someone who has read my poems long since
I would want to say, to her or him,
that my treasure-island is a name
one hundred and eighty miles
from transparent Saharan waters.
Volcano amid black lava
where misty roads climbed,
my island had white villages
with squares surrounded by balusters
and the small neoclassical bandstand for concerts.
The volcano dropped away steeply
on its northern slope down to the valleys
with green banana plantations to the sea.
Towards the south it sloped more gently
to desert terrains as far as the beaches
where today pipelines disgorge
sunblock-cream and beer.

My island is a rubbish dump
for feelings where I have buried the affection
that I gave up for lost, and every line
that I have written is part of the treasure-map.
To find the coast again
I would have to sail through time
as far as that intimate and colonial city
that used to tend towards calm and silence,
with women leaning their arms on cushions
over the window-sills
and Indianos chatting in cafés.

Memory makes muted transcriptions
of those voices lost
around the Christmas of 'fifty-two.
From high windows we gazed down mid-morning
at the square with its Indian laurel,

the music from the bandstand, the empty guagua
and the conductor and the driver drinking
a glass of wine at the bar with its marble top.
Above the Indian laurel, the port could be seen
with its ships and cranes. Higher up,
like a dark blue curtain, hung the sea
with another island in the background, mauve-coloured.
It was a time together that each one keeps to himself
for bouts of depression under the rain.
The instant of years. Our clear shadows
against the light in front of the windows.
I left on a cargo ship crossing the Atlantic
to reach this bigger port of Barcelona.
I left in order to learn to read
the future in the cracks of houses
as though they were the lines of a hand.
Somewhere there is still my shelter
of the square, the voices, the big windows,
and this present of today, which was then
tomorrow hidden behind the frieze of the sea.

Moon of the island, buoy of the past,
nights of the hemisphere with the volcano and the sea;
the swarm of lights of the refinery,
with the tankers just off the coast
as though they were already sailing to oblivion.
A scent of ancient dominions came
from that melodious castilian,
from the shipping trade with England,
from the dark-skinned Indians in their bazaars,
from the Botanic Garden crossed
by avenues of sugar-cane
which the trade-winds passed through
as though through a hair-sieve.
The one who lives there never recognises
a treasure-island.
There still remain the memories of propeller-planes
aluminium-coloured, on the concrete runway
of an airport perpetually closed by fog,
black and white photos of those days,
climbing by mule up to the lonely
crater that has never been profaned
by tourists queuing for a cable-car.

I search among so many lost names –
maybe already dead – for the addresses of friends
and I phone them on the wind
talking with the flames in the stove
in front of the dark window-panes.
It was a propeller-plane, a four-engine –
silver fish above a sea of clouds –
that brought me nearer to the island with the pure
snow-covered volcano of my adolescence.
A guagua jolted me all the way to the sea,
cutting across the smell of fish hung up to dry,
in front of the small black beach.
Everything happens on the other side of my years,
these dark and heavy boots
that have carried me so far from myself.

There is nothing else but the night: there is no sea,
nor music from the very first pick-ups,
nor am I there either,
I cannot phone you, understand this.
Outside there are the wild boar, the night birds;
they cross the ploughed fields soundlessly,
they see a light in the house, and to give it a wider
berth, they broaden the arc of their path.
With the treasure-island you have to do the same,
keep yourself at a distance from this danger
that with its beauty threatens us.

# Initiation

Narrow streets and sad street-corners,
signs on balconies advertising
the cure of venereal disease, cheap douches for men.
Histories of love, permanganate and dawn.
The first woman
in a room with icy sheets.
The moon wears the face
of that poor whore in Madrid.
The city grey, like the police.
It was a mythical, clandestine journey.
I don't want to turn it into an epic.
It didn't mark me nor did I feel dirty.
Only a preliminary trial:
in order to accustom myself to this mystery
which unites, within me, my love for you
with a danger of dark alleyways.

# Poem in black

It's a tired district, a hopelessness
of unpainted houses, from which emerge big,
big-bellied men who always shout, unkempt women,
children with a star of impetigo on the mouth.
It's a place of syringes, of graffiti on walls
and plastic blowing in the wind: city of oblivion,
far from the other well-lit, famous streets,
the streets of big business and rendezvous of lovers.
Stucco with no cement, here life falls down
and there are no noble cracks. A radio at full volume,
shatters silences of dry drains.
Suddenly, out of a doorway steps someone in disguise
with painted face, a huge cardboard nose
and a scarlet cloak. Then, in an instant,
the district is its own saddest grimace.
Grotesque, the carnival wants to cheat death,
and disguises with fear an even blacker fear.
The mask always hides another darker mask
of the self, the hardest, solitary mannikin.

# Paintings from an exhibition

We have always gone back to Paris together, you and I.
The *Estació de França* stays behind –
a pile of iron in the night – like the past.
The moon is bluish seen from the train,
the moon made from memories of shadow
like, for me, the Paris of thirty years ago
in your eyes
                              – the eyes of that girl, I mean:
literature, exile, the French *chanson*.
We were young, we went in search of the rainy
cities with slated mansard roofs,
the below-zero cities of great wars
and great poets. They made us feel like heroes,
                                                  political, cultured,
in pursuit of a literature
that has ended for ever. Sartre sleeps
in the grey autumn of Montparnasse,
near Baudelaire, the withered flowers
and the page torn from a notebook of an unknown woman,
the handwriting half-erased by the rain.
Now we are able to understand that dark green
of Cézanne's shadiest corners
and the rainy light of Montparnasse
under the tall chestnut trees with their naked branches,
where Simone de Beauvoir,
like all those of that time, is also already asleep,
in the exhibition of paintings of shadow.

We have always gone back to Paris together, you and I.
And now that it is one hundred years since Cézanne,
what does it mean for him, the painting
of the bridge, which you like so much?
In a warm room we look at
the white cloth on which apples tumble, red,
                              green, blue: our youth.
All the landscapes of this luminous green,
what are they inside their shadow without paintings?
With the mauve gaze of the *joueurs de cartes*
and with the black, mistrustful eyes

of his self-portraits,
Cézanne looked one day at this deepest
green lake of darkness
that we look at among paintings and whispers
under the dim lights of the *Grand Palais*:
a woman who is over fifty
and a man of sixty search for new nostalgias.
We go back to the metro which, without our realising it,
has been modernising its rolling-stock.
It's already hard to hear Léo Ferré,
but it's still the Paris rain.
In a small hotel with a terrible name –
                              Hôtel de l'Avenir –
beside the darkness, vast as a Cézanne,
of the Luxembourg Gardens' obscure green,
on a November night in ninety-five,
I write this poem.

## Etching

Bullets of hail strafe the panes,
squalls lash the pavements.
And you and I are here, where the bad weather
summarises the obstacles which sometimes
have brought us to the edge of the abyss.
Eyes shining with faults and hands burnt
through having grabbed the frozen iron
of hell's handrail to save ourselves.
Let fate continue shooting
for no good reason, as usual, at the window-panes.
Nothing makes any sense except our love.

# Autumn path

The male blackbird with dark wings
has received us like an old god of the harvest.
The young wine sits on the table-cloth,
in a bottle that catches the light, rosy
as the fortune-teller's crystal-ball.
In it can be seen – between the rows of vines – a path
with the footprints that you and I leave,
together and on our own.
We are inside the coldness of the glass. When I touch it
we vanish, but you smile at me, real,
on the other side of the white table.
The bottle between us two – our life –
has the light of the setting sun, which is that of the dawn.

# Dark Night in Balmes Street

Threats and fears fulfilled –
all streets lead to old age –
I go past the clinic where you were born,
twenty-six years ago now, on a dark night
wounded by the light of a corridor.
Here you came, small and defenceless,
to the gentle beach of your smile,
to the difficulties with speech,
to the schools that did not want you,
to the bones' weariness, to the cruel
and obvious calm of the corridors
watched over by silent white coats
with the cold murmur of angels.
Twisted thumbs, a nose like a bird's beak,
the lines in your hand confused:
our own features and those too of the syndrome,
as though you had had another, unknown
mother hidden in the garden.
A far cry from intelligence, from beauty;
now only goodness matters,
the rest are questions of an inhospitable world
from which it is hard to hide ourselves
in rare flights of happiness.

I go back to that dark garden that I was gazing at
from the coffee-machine,
sole companion of those early mornings.
I go back to the blame and the remorse,
old fields of rubble I am still crossing:
my hands refused
to do what I wanted. How I respect
the wisdom of my hands,
that turned against me
and dragged me by my neck towards old age,
forcing me to look at the morning
on which, facing me squarely,
your tenderness just saved you.
Old misunderstanding of what happiness is,
and the world around me, neither friend nor foe:

I gaze at the crowds in the streets,
the building-works, the offices, enquiring
into tears that are lost.

You are the flower, we the branches,
and the gust of wind, stripping your petals,
left us naked, shaking with grief.
I still protect you and passing so close
to the garden, so dark, that summer,
I lean out and see once more that feeble
light from the coffee-machine.
Twenty-six years. And I know that I am happy
and that I've had the life I deserve.
Never could I be something
different from her, chance and fire.
A chance for life, fire
for death, for not even having a tomb.

## A woman speaks

Look at all those weary sunsets inside me
and songs unlearned.
Yesterday's colours don't forsake me,
nor the colours of memories, of things we've said
scattered in the night.
Mystery of love. Out of what tedium
does it come, that courtesy of yours, that serene
attitude towards the abyss of desire?
From where does your voice come, calm and severe,
your hand pointing through the fog?
If they have never defeated you, if things we've said
are contour-lines on some map
of lost feelings.
If being right has never succeeded
in making me fall in love with you,
then surely we could exchange
half of being right and calm and sensible
for just one spark of mystery.

# Sonnet in two cities

*Le rouge pour naître à Barcelone, le noir pour mourir à Paris.*
LÉO FERRÉ: Thank you, Satan

*Hôtel de l'Avenir*, the final night:
Paris shows off her evening through the glass.
What luck to be approaching sixty –
my *Porte des Lilas* – wearing a smile.
What luck not to have been a sad man,
nor you a sad woman. Hurts
toughen us, make us compassionate.
What luck these two daughters. And this son.
What luck to be able to see, beyond the glass,
a city that does not exist, our own:
Ferré sings Verlaine, and the rain lays
its red and black reflections on the night.
Red for being born in Barcelona,
black for the night-trains to Paris.

# The combination

On my own between two hells –
that of liberty and that of age –
I cannot open our safe.
The door with its rotating numbers
is the roulette where I no longer know how to lay bets:
from the very first sighs I have kept
armour-plated the light of that rose.
In our bedroom, naked,
with the light out and the window open,
I feel the urban freshness of the night
while a light breeze caresses me.
That girl I was and the boy you were
remain very close, they are within me:
a familiar smell, a song,
release them, but, when I want to speak to them,
they have already vanished.
We lived at the mercy of what we didn't know
about ourselves,
as though life held, among its rights,
a mysterious right of not knowing.
The metallic nest guards our dreams.
I am weeping: the combination
was the date of your death.

# Son in winter

The train pulled up before dawn
in the empty station.
We walked feeling the icy air
along dark deserted streets
until the first café switched on its lights.
There we waited until it was day
for the Maternity Hospital to open its doors to us.
In a single early morning we became rich:
within us we can still see
how the sun rises among narrow streets
and the cribs in rows in the half-light.
Today that infant
is a jazz musician. While I listen to him
playing his sax in a club of *Ciutat Vella*,
at the back of the stage are the lights
of the misted-up windows of a night-train
or of a café at dawn: the dim light
that is kept burning there where
timidly our love for him began.

# Immigrants

To me the Rambla seems hostile: they are there
in the stench of the leftovers in the Boqueria market,
like a flock marked with poverty, cattle
covered in mud and flies, fearful religions.
Everything is a dirty gold: the pavement of the Rambla,
like a tomb of the crowd,
façades of stucco with light from the sea.
They will never be relegated to the background.
I immerse myself in contagions, along streets
whose walls have buckled, flaking,
in fumes of frying food and the stench of filthy water,
mould's beautiful emerald
spreading from the base of the fountain,
the parked cars,
with their number-plates from years ago,
asparagus-ferns on balconies, glowing
amid the melancholy of rust.

Would it have been better not to have left the place
where they were born, with its folklore of dead children,
and weevils in empty jars of flour?
Or to search for a place where poverty
resembles a future, to fulfil one's dream
of being like a stranger version of ourselves?
I have seen the dark glow in their eyes:
it is difficult to decide once and for all
that we are at home.

They will inherit the Rambla, the flower-stalls,
the Universities and their clamour,
the smell of the sea in the evening air
on the café terraces. The cafés too,
the hospitals, the banks,
the hillier districts with their luxury flats.
They will inherit the squares and the streets,
the beaches, the law courts,
the autumn rains, when they will remember
small, spoiled fruits on grey trees,
the bustle of early mornings at work,

the desolate metro stations at dusk.
They are still the wake of hostile tongues
in a strange and even crueller land,
who dreamed of a map crossed
by trains that never came back.
Mountains of the past, ancestors who with pride
will one day shine like black jewels
in a conversation in an easy-going place
which will still perhaps be called,
or which no one will ever again call *fatherland*.

# Last train
*(Collserola crematorium)*

If you could see the rain varnishing
the dark green thicket of this garden.
Your carriage now arrives all alone
in this spacious room, with no fittings,
no lamps lit, no furniture,
death's *Estació de França.*
All that can be heard is the gentle hum
of the motor that slowly draws
this load of childhood,
youth and the lost, anonymous years
that no one will ever reclaim,
towards the incandescent mouth of the oven
reflected in the big rainy window.
Tears adorn this place
that's ugly as a suburb and, in spite of everything,
I retrieve you from a blue morning
beneath the plane trees, one far-off winter:
with your hands behind your back, stock-still,
you gaze at the crowd among the kiosks
of the Rambla, like a survivor
who strains to identify
from his surroundings
the remains of the shipwreck.

# Dawn at *Cap de Creus*

You have waited for me so sadly.
In front of the purple rocks
flocks of gulls watch over you,
lyric seekers after carrion
in the grey hardness, dead man's head
raised up by the pure light off the sea.
I edge along the wall that drops dizzily down,
I look over the precipice
and, as always, you offer me
a poisonous and indifferent silence.
I have lived postponing the threats
of winter in my eyes
ever since a child, who found at your feet
the huge, deep-blue drawing-room of the most learned sea.

Like a forehead the cape spreads out
over the sea the whole of our history.
Buffeted by the north wind, I have come alone
so as not to have to pretend to the feeling
for beauty that I lost long ago.
This path printed on stone
is the last stage of my journey,
the one that runs along the edge of the abyss.

# At the hearing

In the small courtroom,
above the glassed-over roof of grey light
the rain beats down just like the sea.
A foot is jerking impatiently.
The worn, black looking-glasses of the gowns
reflect guilt.
The law does not look on the strange as strange
and down in the basement it keeps
the proofs and evidence of conviction
like the goods in a draper's shop;
piles of deeds
tied up with the ribbons of death.
The rain weighs heavily, murmuring
that goodness is common, and wickedness personal.
It is growing dark: the gowns flap
like huge bats at dusk.
We all share the physiognomy of the guilty
and an old look of the prosecution.

# Philosopher in the night

When the darkness of the small hours in Madrid
is behind the panes in O'Donnell Street,
I rest my head upon your absence.
I have opened the *Iliad*. Horned Apollo
is passing like the night and, in time with his steps,
the arrows in his leather quiver rattle.
I feel how cold your place is, where there is no one.
Undressing, I talk as though you were here:
a habit from the first days without you.
The bathroom mirror, without your bottles,
reflects only how old I am becoming.
I carefully fold my clothes and put on my pyjamas
with the grey dressing-gown tied tightly round my body,
and slippers on my old man's feet.
I love your absence beside me,
always closer when I go back to the *Iliad*,
as though the distant echo of the truth
from that beach brought you nearer.
Your shadow and I have raised the girl
and the two boys: only yesterday I had
a letter from the older one. They barely remember you.
I am their Homer in our *Iliad*.
Far from that warm sea with its avenues of plane trees
where we met, I still sense within me
no other Helen but you.
And the past is close by. Like the wind in the black
trees of the *Retiro* in front of my apartment.
The sight of Hector, dressed as a warrior,
frightens his child. The despairing noise
of a motor-cycle has cut across the night.
I too with the bronze of my loneliness
perhaps used to frighten our children.

Your photograph, with its sepia tint,
is on the table, lost among the books:
youthful distance with a sad smile.
Achaeans and Trojans, like a broken sea
of shields and helmets, of wooden spears
tipped with bronze, are sitting on the ground

beside the evening sea which roars at the beach.
But I feel absent: while Ajax hurls himself
against Hector's shield, I think of our sea,
unspoiled as at Troy, of the Costa Brava
in the sixties. I open the big window.
Today that daughter and those sons live far away.
They are older than you: you left so young.
With melancholy I think to myself that now it must be
getting dark in Chicago. And it's the small hours
in Berlin and in the green outskirts of London.
And the only dawns that wait for you are these
that come out at night between words.

While the bonfires blockade the ships
I have appalling thoughts, like the wine-dark sea
that spews up black seaweed on the wet sand.
It happens as though Homer's gods existed.
It's so long ago: you, dead; me, growing old
alone with the *Iliad*. But down there on the beach,
between two battles, while the stars
make the sky blacker, you sleep, like Helen,
beside me, in your darkness.
My eyelids are heavy like the bronze helmet
of a weary warrior who is remembering
Pedralbes and the evening sky, so blue,
in the springtime of that city.
As thin as the ideal line of Euclid
is the *Iliad*'s mythic territory
that we're reading together – you in my life,
I in your death. The philosopher in me emerges
when I see how Achilles has chosen glory
instead of life. Ethics begins:
already in the *Iliad* there is the noble and ancient
lesson of grief, when Hector and his men
come to the boats looking for blood.
There is always an Achilles waiting in the dark.
I think that absence – like river water once used
for tempering weapons – has forged me more strongly.
Each one of us has sensed in his or her own *Iliad*
how weapons crash down on gleaming helmets
and the horrible cries of the Greeks amid the fire
defending their ships. Alcathouos on the ground:

the lance – stuck in his heart – quivering
with his last heartbeat. You will be the lance
that trembles with my body's last desire.
Empty chariots run all over the beach,
and the tiny rustle a leaf makes, as they pass,
is like a feeble ghost of your presence.
Meanwhile, in the window-panes, the park's horizon
begins to lighten, as though there shone
behind the black trees the weapons of Achilles.

How I have searched for you always. And how often
have I disembarked on rugged coasts,
simply because of a light. I open the window
and the dawn of birds in the park greets me.
Hard old age leaves in the eyes
a long beach like the ones in the *Iliad*.
Rusty merchant ship, in front of a big port
I will slice through the foul-smelling waters where thousands
of seagulls are flying, in search of a motionless,
solitary woman who is waiting on the dock.
Today, when the prow is wearily sinking
and the sailor cannot see clearly from afar,
the coast rubs itself out. Gazing at the waves,
I remember your eyes with their evening light
and I think with a smile how I carry your grey,
romantic figure, the iron ship of the soul.

# No return address

The hard part of the journey begins.
We have left the *Estació de França* behind,
under the sky of a lost city.
Now that train is running already a long way from there.
It advances more and more deeply amid the snow.
With my hand I rub the steamed-up windows
and through the fog I see the curved chains
and the iron towers like memories.
From time to time, the dull gleam
of yellowish headlights along a road:
perhaps behind some of them you were travelling.
We are all travelling across what first Eliot
and afterwards Cernuda called
the desolation of the chimera.
This train does not burnish the same rails
twice, I think to myself, my eyes
aware of the rosy warning of the sun
that is setting behind an icy wood.
Everything can yet be saved: love grows
at the hands of this ferocious stimulus
which is the clear certainty of death.

# Ghosts of the barbed-wire

*Rupert Brooke, Wilfred Owen, Edward Thomas,*
*Alfred Lichtenstein, August Stramm, Georg Trakl,*
*Ernst Stadler...Fallen in the First World War.*

Poets who could be my sons,
all dying when young. War
gave them, these innocents, a harsh
cabaret voice and boots for the mud.
Good companions for weather such as now,
so glacial towards poetry,
which goes on burning like the furious
neon beacon of a duty chemist.
Poets who wrote with the calm and,
at the same time, intent gaze of the hunter,
seeking the cold light, intense and hard,
that a poem casts over the world.
Poets for whom life came first
always, before literature.
Sometimes, behind their lines,
I hear the iron echo of the hexameters
of the *Iliad*'s fierce captains.

# You arrived too late for your own time

*You arrived too late for your own time.* Harsh words
which I still feel like a defeat.
But today I don't know what battle
or which time was mine. It is a shame
to be no one, to have boarded the wrong
train, to be left with no suitcase;
asleep in your seat, to go by without stopping
and now to find yourself without clean clothes,
tired, in a seedy hotel with only one
unlucky star, which must be mine.
I shall do without everything except the poet
who survives the disaster. We will disclose
that I have even got the century wrong:
that will be Paris and I Verlaine.

*from*

# JOANA
(2002)

# There are no miracles

It was raining halfheartedly.
At nine o'clock at night – October the nineteenth –
Joana arrived frightened at the operating-theatre
surrounded by the rest of us, who stayed behind
in the small, feebly-lit room beside the lifts.
He told us that, in a desperate effort
to save herself, she said *I love you* to the surgeon.
We were waiting for the good fairy to restore to us
the calm Joana, the one we'd always known,
her eyes sparkling with trust.
At eleven o'clock, as we gazed through the window,
drops of rain were sliding down the glass
as though they were sliding down the night.
Night was the blade of a scythe.

# The dawn at Cádiz

A foggy ocean in front of the hotel.
The long lines of grey foam
sketch out a barrier reef
in front of the balustrade along the beach.
I have heard your name uttered
in the language of the sea. It says you are going away.

The solitary black storks repeat it
as they glide over the water.
I'll never know what it is you know about me,
nor in what truth we have been together. It can't be
a bad pain, the pain that comes from you
via this murky sea. December. The last
December with you. And afterwards to search
inside myself for your lost voice.

# Christmas lights at Sant Just

### I

Shivering bulbs light up
just like someone's tears.
I gaze out at our courtyard under the lilac-
coloured sky of evening where, against
the light, the laurel leaves are drawn
in a sharp, black print. Your mother tells me:
*You and I, now and then, we lose everything.*
The Christmas lights are shivering in the streets:
Suddenly, for you, they've all gone out.

### II

Today all the colours inside fairytales,
like the greens of reeds beside the river
and the clouds reflected in the old washing-trough,
are shining in Joana's eyes.
It starts to rain and, over there, across
the yard, it's Christmas of the year before,
with figures moving. I see Joana laugh,
but all at once she turns her head towards me,
stares, and then I know that it's a memory,
because the rain is falling through her.

# Four o'clock in the morning

The first dog starts to howl, and straightaway
there's an echo from a yard
and others sound at the same time in a hoarse
barking devoid of any rhythm.
Lifting their muzzle to the sky, they bark.
Where have you come from, dogs?
What future does this nightly baying call up?

Tonight I hear you
barking my daughter's dream
from your lairs, surrounded by the droppings
with which you mark your territory
of house corners, yards, alleyways.
Just as I'm doing tonight with these poems,
out of which I howl and howl,
and mark out the territory of death.

## Fontana Metro

It was already dark, all the narrow
streets off the *Gràcia* were strung with Christmas
lights and were filling up with people.
There was no room in the bars, the young men and women
were laughing; we were surrounded by the overcoats,
the smiles, the shop windows, the street-lamps.
Couples shooting past on scooters
with their faces hidden inside their helmets.
Joana kept popping up everywhere:
everywhere I met the glance
of that deformed body
from which I learned what beauty was.
Night's mirrors reflected back
her smile for us, that smile spread out
over the last thirty years around us.
I asked: *What are you doing here, Joana?*
From every place she replied: *I'm going away*
*to shatter your life once more.*

## Mother and daughter

Your hands are her entire past:
thirty years of love held in your palms.
You have watched over her the whole night through
and you lie down on the bed beside her,
with your breast against her back
and your face rubbing her tired hair.
You hug her and you talk softly
while you caress her.
These are the final nights. You feel the heat
of her worn-out body you know so well.
In death you will learn how to take care of her.
She has always been a child: watch over her sleep,
which is coming to look more and more, and more,
like the deep dark of joy
in which she is falling, into your hands.

# Plea

Away from this winter morning fine and mild,
please, don't go,
but in this courtyard stay, submerged
like a wreck, inside our life.
Between the bay tree and the aspidistras
with their broad, green, romantic leaves,
please don't go, don't go away.

All is set up so you can carry on,
so stay, then, please, don't go away.
Just tell me you remember: I need
some words that have the deep, clear
voice of absence so I can ask you
about your fleeting triumph over the *never more*.
But you are quiet, resting in the past,
that bed of flashing sadness.

And so you went, shutting yourself inside
the bud of darkness during these eight months,
until today when, terrified by light,
death's pale and furious moth
comes flapping out.

But if you're dying, you are still alive,
and I make the final happiness
unfold across your tired face
with your small hands clasped in mine.
To be dying is to be still alive, I tell myself.
This winter morning fine and mild,
please, don't go, don't go away.

# Final stroll

Already I wasn't eating, my hair was falling out,
I had my eyes shut all day.
But, early in the morning, I was on the balcony
and someone among the trees on the street was speaking to me
in a voice that sounded like my mother's voice,
who lay sleeping in the bed beside mine.
Suddenly I left off being tired
and went down to the street without my crutches:
I had never been able to walk like this,
I felt happiness come back:
illness was a sweaty skin
that I now let fall in the street.
Never had I felt so light.
I looked back at my balcony,
the iron bars like a music-stave,
and I said goodbye to my father and mother.

Life chose me for its love.
Death, as well.

## One poor instant

Death is nothing more than this: the bedroom,
the afternoon luminous in the window,
and on the bedside table this radio-cassette-player
that has stopped like your heart,
with your songs sung for ever.
Your last breath lingers
within me, still suspended: I don't let it end.
Do you know what the next concert's to be, Joana?
Do you hear the children playing in the schoolyard?
When this afternoon is over,
Do you know what the night will be like, the spring night?
People will come.
And the house will put on all its lights.

*2 June 2001*

# End

This was the message of your goodness:
to be buried one spring morning.
Today no one would dare to push
the wheelchair for the last time.
Nothing better than the din
of our city around you
and, in front, the eternity of the sea.
And what a rough prow Montjuïc is,
that goes as far as thought could wish.

Sandy paths
up which the hearse climbs and, behind it,
the cars crunching on gravel at the foot
of the cypresses in the calm square of morning.
I feel your smile that passes through
the clear birds of the air, now that everything
goes back to the beginning, as when you were not.

A scent of flowers lingers at the foot of the wall
among dark, fleeting greens.
The light, sunlit songs of your silence
shine on the iron of the future,
and my words about you
have no more meaning than the rusty
lock of a door that does not open on anywhere.

# June night

When I came out of the cinema it was already dark.
In the old unlit car-park I climbed
the rough and grimy ramp
because I had parked on the terrace roof.
It was a steep slope, like the one inside me:
these were the first days without you.
But when I reached the top, out in the fresh air,
I found myself in a warm silence
surrounding the shadows of a few cars:
reddish floor-tiles, railings
with simple, delicate, iron bars
and tin-cans filled with hydrangeas.
As I came out into the open, a veil
was suddenly torn apart and there appeared the night
of the inside yard of a block of houses
with its verandahs and windows all lit-up.
I stopped
feeling that you were nearby. Feeling that now,
at any moment, I could make death's
treasures appear.

# Space and time

And all at once the house is too big.
Your mother and I have emptied your cupboards,
searching on tables and shelves, and in photograph
after photograph, for your smiles.
At night, with the lights on, the mirrors
show me your empty space in high relief.
The furniture is darker,
and down the staircase comes
the warm banister that remembers
your small hand and the stairs
that still hear your footsteps.
This house, big and empty, stares and stares
at its own silence.

## Children's story

Don't say a word, Joana.
just listen and don't say a word.
It was a rainy morning, we were walking
through the sleeping village, and we entered the heart of it
via a street paved with flagstones that led nowhere.

But there were children shouting and singing
because, approaching the canal, we could see
their house reflected in the water.
How you enjoyed seeing the children, do you remember?
As we walked on, behind us,
their little faces remained at the window-panes
with their voices fading over the water.
We arrived too late, so late,
that we'll always have to go home separately:
that's the price for being able to step inside a story.
And what luck now to find you here,
on this early morning turned courtyard,
because it means that all the time you were
by my side in the darkness.

# Passenger

In the huge airport window
a dawn of white light through the mist
rises up in front of the girl who carries
a book she'll never be able to read.
She carries my youth
inside the bible-thin pages
of this thick, leather-bound volume
of nineteenth-century Russian writers.

Natashas and Nastenkas, my silent
girlfriends from whom I learned
to look for small hopes
as though they were shells on the beach:
through the snow and blizzard I picture you
still hoping to see how some shadow of love
might arrive wrapped-up against the cold.

The motionless girl, too, in her wheelchair
knows that I'll never arrive.
She lifts her eyes to the nostalgic fuselages
of the planes that seem to rest
like seagulls in front of a frozen sea.
My dear friends, make my daughter welcome
because for her I am already faceless:
my face is nothing more than a big airport-
window lit by those white nights.

# Lullaby

Sleep, Joana. May the *Loverman*, tragic, dark,
of that soprano sax
your brother played in the solace of Montjuïc
keep you company through eternity
down the pathways music knows so well.
Sleep, Joana.
And if it may be don't forget your years
in the nest you left within us.
We shall grow old keeping safe all the colours
that shone in your eyes.
Sleep, Joana. This is our house,
everything is lit by your smile.
It is a peaceful silence where we hope
to round off the stones of grief
so that everything you were may become music,
the music which shall fill our winter.

# The present and Forès

### I

Summer morning among the fields.
Mariona is in the garden,
apron on, digging under the rose-bushes.
Mònica – twelve years old – on her bicycle
on the way to the village
and the two youngest, Carles, Joana –
five – are still asleep.
The holiday air shines:
through the open window and into the trees,
among the leaves that the breeze is stirring,
comes the piano of the *English Suites*,
and suddenly I feel sorrow and fear,
as if this order were the huge yawn
with which the future devours us.

### II

Thirty years later there can be heard
through the open window
the piano playing the *English Suites*.
She is still taking care of the roses.
The air, as it does every summer, lulls the house.
I seem to see, far off, the bicycle
making its way to the village, while I think
the two youngest are asleep upstairs.

But Mònica is in Barcelona
with her children, Carles on his travels,
and Joana is dead.
A strange blend of that time,
calm as the sunken hull of a wreck,
and a violent, fleeting time inside my head.

### III

I try to remember, but the spaces
where nothing now remains are too big.
It is so empty, memory's mirror:
brief, extinguished flares, because the big
authentic memory is death.
There all the lost moments will be
building the garden with no one in it,
the empty house, the sun at the windows,
timorous life
like a fleeing bird that crosses
the stage-set of oblivion.

# Professor Bonaventura Bassegoda

I remember you as tall and fat,
obscene and sentimental: you were then
an authority on Deep Foundations.
You always began our class
with the words: *Gentlemen, good morning. Today*
*it is so many years, so many months, and so many days*
*since my daughter died.*
And you used to wipe away a tear.
We were in our twenties,
but the sight of you, a big fat man
weeping in front of the class,
never roused a smile from any one of us.
How long is it since you stopped counting the days?
I have thought of you and of all of us
now that I am your bitter shadow,
because for my daughter
it is two months, three days and six hours
that she has in death her deep foundation.

# First summer without you

### I

Greenish-grey cliffs sink
into the water like huge prehistoric axes.
As though peeling a piece of fruit,
the road gives one twist then another
round old burnt hills.

The car has stopped beside the beach
without your eyes in the rear-view mirror.
In front, painted in white, there is *La Gambina*,
with the sign – HOTEL – in blue
up on the roof looking out towards the future.

### II

You sit down beside the waves:
the clouds pile up over the village,
but you are facing the horizon,
under the sky of the past, our best time.
The sea, the people, the boats, everything's moving
in this last postcard of you.
The wind rehearses gusts
that carry off some flying parasol.
Cold drops of rain
on hot skin
are like a warning by mothers
gathering up the shadow of danger in the eyes
on a beach abandoned to the wind.

### III

Joana, the storm
is licking beneath your tired feet.
I see you escaping with your slow pace
crossing the rain's glance.
Suddenly, you're neither at home nor on the beach
and all the photos of you where you are smiling
are being battered by the north wind of terror.

For many years your crutches were thrust
among the pebbles to carry you right down to the sea.
Under the iron bridge –
the dead swallows will tell you this –
your beloved village of Colera
will never change any more in your eyes.

# Gravestone

ANNA (1967), JOANA (1970-2001)

> *In our memory your names*
> *have remained on a little beach*
> *that is not listed on ships' charts.*


Here, how close you are, one to another,
my daughters, after such a long time.
Both of you together, behind your names
that gaze out to sea
and which the sun reads each break of day.

# Waiting

So many things are missing you.
Each day is full of moments that are waiting
for the small hands that, so many times,
grasped my own.
We have to get used to your absence.
A summer has already gone by without your eyes
and the sea too will have to get used to it.
Your street, for a long while yet,
will be waiting in front of the door,
patiently, for your footsteps.
Nor will it ever tire because, when it comes
to waiting, nobody does it as well as a street.
And I am brimful of willingness
to be touched by you, looked at by you.
And please tell me what I should do with my life,
while days of rain or clear blue skies
are already arranging loneliness.

# In the depth of the night

It is freezing outside.
Even the nightingale is silent.
With my forehead pressed against the glass
I ask my two dead daughters
to forgive me
because I hardly ever think about them.
Time has gone by leaving dry clay
on top of the scar. And, even
when you love someone, forgetfulness sets in.
The light has the hardness of the drops
that fall from the cypresses with the thaw.
I put another log on and, poking the ashes,
draw a flame from the embers. I make coffee.
Your mother comes out of the bedroom
smiling: *That smells good.*
*You're up early this morning.*

*from*

# STRUCTURAL
# CALCULATIONS
(2005)

# Self-portrait with sea

It's that quiet child who plays by himself.
He's behind these old man's eyes
resisting the onslaught of noon,
listening to the waves' confused verses
and the cries of naked, rusting bodies
entering cold clear water
on that stony beach. He is ashamed,
and goes from one tale's hiding-place to another.

Sleep within me, lost child:
Sleep within me on a Three Kings night
when broomsticks fly in silence
and wolves leave paw-prints in the snow.
Outside, the sky fills up with apricots
and the sea, the deep blue of plums,
breaks open on the rocks' black knives.

This summer with freezing alcohol in my eyes
I feel my black and yellow life
like the flesh of a fruit that is rotting
around memory's stone.
Hide within me, lost child.
Inside me, sheltered from noon,
tell the story about the grey boy
and the miserable bicycle
that the sad cyclist of the suburbs rides.
He's searching for you and is now quite close.

# Young partridge

It was crouching in a furrow, and when I picked it up,
it felt as though your hand was in mine.
There were patches of dried blood on one wing:
the tiny bones, like ribs,
were shattered by buckshot.
It tried to fly but, trailing the wing,
could scarcely drag itself along the ground
before hiding beneath a stone.
I still feel that warmth in my hand,
because a fragile creature gave meaning
to each of my days. A fragile creature
likewise now beneath a stone.

# Feeble brightness

The bubble of light within the tunnel
carries our faces away with it into the dark.
Although I recognise some trace
of that war-time child corrupted
by the gloomy myth of purity,
I look at myself in the glass of the metro carriage
with a mineral indifference,
because I already know that nothing inside me will change.

An old man's love is as hard as the fig tree
with its dusty, horribly contorted limbs, his heart
is dark and hidden, like the heart of the rose
among its crimson petals that are big but weak.
Cold passion is even more blind.
Sex puts up a fight in a hovel
with hardly any light, at the back of your mind.
Outside, death waits to come in.

# Writings and rooms

Father Hopkins S.J. finished writing
*The Wreck of the Deutschland*
at St Beuno's College in a green
and idyllic corner of Wales far from the sea
in May eighteen hundred and seventy-six.
The Jesuits can be quite precise
about which room he was staying in when,
starting from a ship that sank
in the North Sea during a storm,
he wrote the mystical poem of the nineteenth century.

Today, nobody knows in which room
Luis Cernuda wrote *The Family*,
that wreck which is like that of the *Deutschland*.
Nobody knows it: nor have the Jesuits
ever found the table-cloths made
from the same altar-cloth
nor any of the panes of glass that reflected back
the well-known supper, presided over
by eyes the colour of fear and hands of wax
for evermore. It's the mystical poem
of the twentieth century: here is the family,
in a blurred and frozen parody of the Last Supper,
plummeting downwards during one of the harsh
and sudden storms during which
history's abyss splits open at our feet.

# On loneliness

While I wander through a street-market,
I'm thinking that, in placing my own chill on poems,
I'm like the archaeologist, in that I try to rescue
the remains of the past as though they were trophies.
Let's say I propose saving
the autumn day when I first met you,
or my very first steel structure,
or the moment we saw our daughter die.
Beside the market, on a building site,
surrounded by plastic bags dragged along by the wind,
a rag-and-bone man is emptying his van
which is stuffed with worn-out trophies:
engraved cups and trays,
figures in rhetorical poses.
I have halted in the face of so much squalor.
The man is scattering it all round him.
Life is made from ignoble metals
that have already lost their shine.
But nothing ages
with less dignity than trophies.

# End of day

Now that you are only
a petal trapped in the amber of not-being,
there must be some place where we can be together,
more together. Maybe in this redoubt
of poems. For what are they
if they cannot save you from oblivion?
In case you come to read them, I'll leave
the book open at night on the table.

# Secrets

Even in bad weather she went out
when it was already dark, after supper,
*and not to be a nurse*, as my father used to say.
She lived in a bigger flat, just above ours
and would always say something pleasant to me
if she met me on the stairs. She even
wanted to teach me to speak French:
I didn't understand what my mother meant
until the following year but, from then on,
they forbade me to speak to her.
We met, even so, I on my way to school,
she on her way home and, in secret.
I'd go with her to the bar where she had breakfast.
Once, on one of those mornings,
she took off her watch and gave it to me
because it reminded her of sad things.
When I got home I too took it off
and hid it behind the electricity meters.
According to her, if I looked at it, I would know
whether the next hour would be a happy one.
Another day she gave me a book
of poems by Campoamor.
She read me 'The express-train': when she finished
she was crying and I felt badly because people could see us.
*When the watch warns you of sadness*
*read this poem, it will make you strong,*
she said, wiping her eyes very carefully.
When that course ended, in June,
I stopped seeing her, until one day,
a day of clear, deepest September blue,
someone found her dead in her bath.
For several days, people in the neighbourhood
spoke of her in an *only to be expected* tone of voice
whose complacency I found terrifying.
Some months later, our family
moved into her flat, now freshly painted
and where no trace of her remained
except for an unpainted hole below the washbasin
where the pipe went into the wall.

From the man I am today to those years
my life stretches back, and I have lost,
sometimes through love, all my houses.
I have never re-read Campoamor,
neither have I covered that hole
through which, abrupt and desolate, and always
secret, the sex of childhood comes back.

## Es Pujol

*On the death of Andreu Alsina, 'Andreu, the Boss'*

We'd sit, when supper was over, in the open doorways
and the geckos would come out in the quiet of the walls.
We were on the very top of the hill
looking out over the roofs of Campanet.
Little by little sleep would hush
the children's happy clamour.
He would talk then, in a soft,
old-fashioned Mallorquin, of the time when he'd go
around the coasts without lights, smuggling.
He has gone off to a night just like those,
and all that had been familiar to us –
the veil of evening on the façades of the houses,
his open doorway, the narrow street,
the hours of the clock's face tolled from the bell-tower –
is now full of mystery. When death comes,
the things we know become
the symbols of things unknown.

# Final struggles

The old man remembers: *it was here,*
*it's this building.* He has stopped
to gaze up at the very top of the façade.
He thinks of the attic's sunlit landing
and the girl with eyes the colour of wood:
a young couple skidding
on hope's frozen bend.
They were bored, both by Franco in the newspapers
and Marx in the underground meetings.
There was a lot of light, and now he recalls
the girl sun-bathing on the terrace
and the husky voice of a French song
under the sky of the past. He remembers too
when they moved to another flat and she
would come here with her lover.

The noise of the traffic is confused and discordant
and it sounds to him like the noise of his own life:
he sees them both in bed and her hand
wandering over his naked body.
The past is a tired red sun
that starts to emerge from the horizon
and now lacks the strength to rise up.
It will never rise again, he's known this for years:
life is a patched-up net
that can never go back to the sea. But when it seems
that there's nothing left, because love
has become for so long this plundering,
there rises up inside him the violent fever
of imagining her in another's arms.
He desires this woman, that girl
he sees inside the attic, who smiles
at him or another, it makes no difference now.

# Morning in Montjuïc cemetery

I have climbed the hill of the tombs.
I have reached this spot by crossing the waste ground
of *Can Tunis*, snowy with plastic bags
and syringes, where junkies wander
shakily about like statues made from rags.
They say the Council wants to bulldoze it,
concrete over these fields of weeds
in front of the huge wrought-iron gate
of the cemetery, that rises in front of the sea.
For the dead it will mean less congenial company:
the dead, their wall and their silence
accord well with the junkies wandering
about like lost soldiers after a defeat.

As I climb up the old path above the port
ships and cranes grow smaller
and the sea spreads itself out. Here,
right at the very top,
you are spared the grief of the world.

# Tango

Sex, which is the hard and hidden
armature of love, kept us apart.
Together we entered the underground:
as we walked along the passages, the warm air
caressed her like a lover.
We went each to our own platform.
I was the first to leave:
I left her for ever,
as though she had thrown herself under the train.

# Safety

The bricklayers at dawn get a fire going
with the remains of plank mouldings.
Life has been a building under construction
with the wind at the top of the scaffolding,
and always facing into the void, because you know
that the man who's installing a safety-net has no net.
What use is it to have gone on repeating
words like love?
Feeble light-bulbs at the end of a line,
memories come on. But I don't want
anyone to feel sorry for me: I find
that easy kind of contempt repugnant.
I need pain against oblivion.
A bonfire lit from scraps of wood
burning beside some scaffolding, is who I am:
a tiny blaze
which, however it may be judged,
no one can deny me ever again.

# Entença Street

Flagship of those streets
on the poor side of the *Eixample* district
with the Butagas bottles on balconies,
the Prison is a bulky mass with dark barred windows.
In a guide to the prisons of the world,
possibly awarded a star,
there is this sinister sky-blue on the walls.
Eternal return, destiny or providence,
what the classics mean is this:
that when fate stirs our lives
and pushes up those who are below and leaves
at the bottom those who were on top, nothing changes.
We are forms of a much deeper disorder.

# Going past the Terramar

Sitges, in the sixties: that old, luxurious hotel
where I wrote the book, *Winter Sea.*

Thirty years later, when it was only a short
time before her death, we went there together:
the paint was already peeling, with the railings
damaged by the sea, and the moquette
worn thin in places by passing feet.

But the glasswork was well-cared for
in those still sumptuous rooms,
separating sitting-room from bedroom,
and made from huge double panes of frosted glass,
with ears of wheat and flowers pressed between them.
That's the way those few days we spent
together there have remained in my memory.
*Perhaps you'll go back with her to the Terramar,*
says the horizon's blue looking-glass.
We, the old, don't look for truth.
Every certainty is nothing more
than a useless wound.

# About my father and mother's honeymoon

Ávila, July nineteen-thirty-six:
he scratched both their names on the ramparts.
The swallows were black bullets
piercing the radiant summer sky
with news of the first deaths.
It's the epic that has stayed with me: years later,
in the midst of the fear I felt as a child,
I learned to keep quiet and dream,
hearing those voices: *You'll have your own war.*

Not one of those who said that to me is left.
I've never carved my name on a stone,
but neither has fear lessened its grip on me,
because life has shown me the faces
of those who could be my murderers.

# Motorway

It's growing dark and in the car
is the sound of Neruda reading his poems.
Amid raucous lorries, the headlights' beam
goes pushing through the rain as though searching
for a child forgotten in her tomb
and for the poem he never wrote for her.
Did he sense, my pathetic and egotistical hero,
on any cold early morning,
that love is not the writing of love poems?
Poor Neruda, poor great poet
weeping under ground for the child
who waited for him in an old graveyard
amid the yellow and lilac fields of Holland.
The poems hid her from sight just as the wind
covers a dead bird with fallen leaves.

# Athens Airport

The rosy-fingered dawn caresses
the fuselage of planes which look, as they take off,
like aluminium ghosts out of the *Iliad*.
The voice of the ruins of some god,
a voice like crumbling ramparts,
trickles in Greek from the loudspeakers.
Next to the bearded, sweaty pope, in robes
of washed-out black, like an icon,
men with the sharp faces of traders
talk and gesticulate with their mobiles.
Bored girls with smooth stomachs
leaf through magazines and queue
in front of half-rusted machines
dispensing soft drinks. Coca-cola:
this is the elixir Helen drinks,
as she displays her bare legs and scarlet-
painted toe-nails, that challenge
anyone proposing to bury the myth.

# Landscape of La Conca
*Solivella, Blancafort*


These are two villages buried among the vineyards.
They cannot see each other: it is their cemeteries
which, from the tops of their hills, gaze at each other from afar.

Your grief and mine hide
as these villages do.
And the daughter we'll never see again
is the one who looks out at us from our eyes.

It is life that is hard to understand, not death.
In death there is no hidden enigma.

## Structural calculations

Already this city does not come with me now,
by my side, to keep me company,
nor do I try to shelter from wind and rain.
All that I thought we were learning then –
the Greek temples, the structural calculations –
when the Diagonal ran across fields
and I was a student of architecture,
is a profession of dead bricklayers
and foundations made of mist. She too,
that warm girl who loved me,
has become the unknown woman
whom I stare at in the photograph of a garden
where she is stretched out in a swimsuit.
A sad desire stirs rebelliously,
and I search for traces of some other love
along the pathway which, between bare legs,
still leads me, weary, to my dream.

So this is how I'm entering old age:
at first it seems as though there are no changes,
like a boat that has turned off its lights
and engine at night, when entering port,
but which carries on in the dark
gliding forward in silence on the water.
Now, although I know that to remember
sex when by oneself is to die alone,
in searching for her lost body,
I calculate my last structure.

# The sons of Captain Grant

On the fly-leaf of the book,
the dedication is still there.
The distinguished explorers gaze at me
from their pen and ink engravings
and I feel how dark it's growing at Turó Park.
From that time on, their sailing ship, the *Duncan*,
never ceased to search the oceans
for the island where the castaways launched their message.
As I read, I was running away from that world
that appeared to be too dangerous,
like girls later, like death now.
With this book, someone
will hurl into tomorrow's hazardous sea
another bottle with a message inside it
that says: don't run away, you'll always come across
some shipwreck or other, because you belong –
like the *Duncan* and Captain Grant –
to the foggy ocean of the real world.

# Shipwrecks

The damp and narrow street is almost blocked
by heaped belongings: rusting refrigerator,
two mattresses propped up against the wall,
a sofa and a standard-lamp, both broken.
All that is left, now, from an eviction.

They're debris from the future.
They're things you often find in streets like these,
but now he's thinking they might be his own
remains, the things he's seen.
He turns: a cat creeps underneath the sofa
and stares at him with green eyes just like hers.

# Bedroom

*Birds never make nests in dead trees,*
I remember you telling me, courageously.
From the room we can see
the shadows the laurel casts like lilac
watercolours on the walls.
Leaves that wither are falling:
only the green ones remain, mottled
by black-spot disease.

It's a secret from the bedroom: happiness
rises up out of grief, like birds
out of the thick greenness of the branches.
Do you remember them singing at Montjuïc
on that June morning? That why the trees
in cemeteries are evergreens.

# End of a tale

The stars that gaze at themselves
in the water of the pond have kept watch over
other lives before this life of ours.

It's a summer night: the pond holds,
more fragile than that of any star,
the reflection of the smile we've lost for ever.
The dogs plunder it,
when they approach and drink the dark water.

# Scene

A young couple are standing beside the bar.
Her lips are brightly painted, her fingernails
are long and beautifully shaped.
He is strong and agile, with a tender expression
and a sparrow-hawk's black eyes. They gaze at each other
and speak softly. Every time they pause
they caress each other with a long smile.

From the bar to the tables it's only a few steps.
Sitting down over there are a couple –
an elderly man and woman – who are silent
and do not look at each other. Outside, an ambulance
goes by like the last trump on Judgement Day.

# Conversation

A memory, impregnated with words
as moquette with dust.
She was telling me where she had been with him,
what they had talked about, how lovely the night had been.
*And have you already slept with him?* I blurted out.
Smiling, and in a tone of voice that credited it
with no importance whatsoever, she answered:
*Of course, heaps of times.*

A conversation we never finished
and her smile today, after all that time.
I'm looking at a photograph
where we're gazing into each other's eyes like a couple in love.
From the date, it was only a few days
before the conversation.
With the years, how strange love can be,
or the memory of it, or the trace
the memory leaves behind, when it dies.

# The age you would be now

Wearing sunglasses and standing beside the sea
I can gaze, from behind my lenses,
at the unmoving horizon of former summers.
The waves breaking echo in the afternoon
like those conversations we've never had.
Behind what breeze, behind what glass
might I glimpse you, huge transparent birds
erased by absence or maybe fallen
under the weight of melancholy.
One year's grain of dust blows in the wind.
But the years don't touch you.
I'm counting birthdays as though measuring
the depth of an ever-deepening well.

# Inventory

A street-light has had its glass smashed
and is out. Its purpose
is not to shed light on the pavement,
but to be an iron post in the darkness.
In the street there is a burnt-out skip,
blackened, with its plastic damaged.
The thing itself, too, is
twisted and capsized, a piece of rubbish.

Our daughter is this anguish
at time passing, time freezing our life.
Now, her purpose is not to love
or be loved, but to be the dust
of grey, insensate material.

Everything loses its fragile purpose.
And look, love, I just don't care
what name we end up giving all this,
because this is where our strength comes from.
This part of me that you know nothing about,
where I keep my cold, intemperate grief,
the part of me you dislike the most, is the part
that has been closest to you, the part of me that
has always, unconditionally, loved you most of all.

# Beirut moon

My foreign correspondent friend
has grown old under the shadow of the wars
in this blackness that is a Phoenician light.
On a hot night, with the haze
veiling that ancient and rusty sickle,
he goes for a stroll along the *Corniche* and gazes at
the shimmering, light-embroidered cloak
of the Christian city on the horizon.
The Arab families on chairs
they've brought out and placed beside the handrail,
talk, eat and laugh
around fishing-rods.
There's a smell of drains, of frying food,
of jasmine, sea and sweat.
From time to time he passes a dented car
with its doors open and the radio
turned up high, and youngsters
gnawing at hot corn on the cob,
cooked on those old travelling carts
wreathed in hot, thick, golden smoke.
He strolls along the *Corniche* and misses
those reasons when he gave his body orders,
always beyond what was wise.
A dark figure, as though straight out of
a tale of Moorish arches and crescent moons,
carries in one hand an enormous coffee-pot
and with the other makes two china cups
clink together just like castanets.
The coffee-vendor has come
from the thousand and one hot, dark nights,
where the machine-gunned walls of the city
open their holes like dark mouths.
All this is familiar to my friend:
he strolls along the *Corniche* and thinks about
what he is running away from and what he has found here,
beside the dangerous pit left by an abstract,
brutal, monotheistic fantasy.
Life goes on gnawing at

the remains of death, just as the diggers
gnaw with their teeth at old Beirut
like the youths their corn on the cob, with the music
now in vogue drifting over the oldest sea in the world.

# The railway bridge

The night-train emerges all lit up
from inside the tunnel and comes on to the iron bridge,
raised high up above the roof-tops,
on stone piles in the midst of the orchards.
It resembles love's fleeting din:
the train is throbbing, just like sex.
It disappears dizzily. All at once
there's nothing but a wind shaking the stem
of a flower between the platforms. If you suffer
from insomnia, it will be good company for you,
this old and solid iron tool.
The bridge cuts across our intimacy.

## Summer's seductions

The stage is in front of the terraces
of the bars, beside the beach.
The moonlight has got brighter
as though it too was part of the show.
Some figures come on and, suddenly,
the music hits us, a voice
seduces us with the vulgarity
of innocence, with those easy rhymes
that bewitch us, and the musicians, the terraces,
the beach, the sea, everything is inside night's
box and, on top, the moon's label.

The sky is full of stars and the bars are closed,
the stage has remained, its old wooden boards,
and the slow, clear-cut, despairing sound
the waves repeat in the night.
The sea, in the darkness,
shines like a horse in its stall.

# Homage

They are sure to blow up the empty bridge
from which the old man stares at the slow waters.
It's not a good place to stop, now
that he's decided to run away from the victors.
It grieves him to leave what he loves behind.
This is not a good place to stop.
They've already passed this way, the ones on the run.
When Hemingway wrote this story
he must have already known that the battle
of the Ebro would take place within himself,
that the old man of the bridge would wait for him forever.

# Asking

She is staring at some point
beyond the window. *What are you thinking?* you ask.
You don't expect any answer: you ask simply
to find out how the words sound
within the ambit of your loneliness.
Asking is dangerous. Memories are now
canisters of poison-gas, abandoned
on old battlefields full of flowers.

# Insomnia

Cruel and lucid, I burn your naked body
in the arms of that man in my memory.
I think of that tonight, beside you,
as you lie fast asleep already, in the half-dark.
I make out the dress on the chair:
there's a black bra on the chair-back,
a stocking dangling, touching the ground
where a pair of shoes lie like fallen birds.
With the light out we are two shadows,
one asleep and the other lying awake.

I have got up and I gaze out at the black laurel
in the freezing December night.
The night that now covers, somewhere or other,
the window behind which
a man is growing old
who, perhaps, no longer remembers you.

The darkness now spreads out over the courtyard
like a mat: the very same darkness
as when we shall all be dead and there no longer remains
a night without love and without stories.

## Two photographs

A girl in a swimming costume smiles
on a grey stretch of beach.
Behind her, the sea in black and white:
the wave has halted on the crest,
just before breaking. It never will.
We will never see its foam.

On the same piece of furniture, a young man
takes a step among the crowd.
Behind him, the plane trees of the Rambla.
Raincoat over his arm, he will never move on:
we'll never know where that step took him.

We've forgotten what was dirty and hard,
all those things that one day were real.
Now they are a reflection in our eyes,
which search for a clue about who we are,
about our own goodness and days gone by.
Those who may look at us will also want to find
the best of themselves in portraits.

## Final notice

You wouldn't recognise the ferocious
neglect that has endured.
I don't want to be docile now I'm growing old,
but being an old rebel is even more pointless.
Lucidity is part of the coldness
and now love is in your silence.
The future is left dumb as a tap
when the pipes have frozen,
and the past writes letters with the rules
of a timetable which it will never observe:
I understand it, but I'm already too tired,
and the old, grimy door, its wood cracked,
which I shall now open, doesn't lead to Paradise.
I prefer music to life.

# The blackbird

At daybreak, black and gleaming, quick and deft,
over the green, damp grass, mistrustful
it disappears in little hops beneath a rose-bush.
Behind the glass, my grief thinks it's her:
my daughter, now under a spell inside a fairytale.
Witch or princess. Maybe Death.

It emerges again: the nervous movements of the head,
the perfect beak, the eyes two hard and shining points.
I approach the glass: it remains motionless
as though it saw the shadow of ivy somewhere else.
It comes back each dawn. It knows I watch it through the window.
Silently, it hops across the lawn, among the tears
of the dew. Under the trees it dodges round stems,
and pecks away at great speed.
It has flown up, suddenly it looks at me from a branch:
she flees from her fairytale, witch or princess. Maybe Death.

It's a blackbird: each year it's a different one.
I'm the one who fantasises, seeking drama, myths and dreams.
Lightly, with my fingers, I tap on the glass:
mistrustful, it flies up again, nimble, astute, real blackbird.

# Venice

Can you feel how, behind the façades
of these palaces, vulgarity
has made its home?
Let's not be survivors, love.
Don't let the dream of this marble or these
rose coloured bricks that peep from under
the shroud of crumbling stucco send us to sleep.
Don't let beauty deceive us a second time:
this streak of mildew looks as though it has flowed
from Bellini's brush, which outlines
the dense olive-greens of the canals,
clogged like the veins of a dead god.
All the palaces are masks, saying:
What are life and poems, without disasters?

# Interior

Both of them go for days on end
with little light, without exchanging a word.
No other dream belongs to them now:
the wind of so many steps towards nowhere
pushes every new step.
Shamelessly, the skeleton reveals itself
beneath the skin: everything that both of them own
is reflected back by each
to the eyes of the other, where nothing shines
now but memory and revenge.
Sitting facing the gloom,
their backs to the window,
they have never been as close as now:
as though it were a question of some great love,
hatred has succeeded in holding in check
even death itself.

# Van Gogh's nephew

He's Theo's son, but he no longer has
any of the paintings – given away or sold off cheap –
of Uncle Vincent's, that are now sought after.
Suddenly he has remembered the rag
he painted for him one day to play with.
He turns everything upside down looking for the sunflower
that is to let him escape from poverty.

I don't know if he found it, but what matters
is knowing that among memory's rags,
among the mistakes and amidst the bad luck,
we still have something valuable. Who knows whether
we shall ever have owned anything as valuable.

## September beach

Beneath the blue tiled vault stretching to the horizon,
there is the clear-cut mosaic of the sea, and the pine woods
shining like dark green bottle-glass:
the postcard of life which, on the back,
in your childish, difficult hand,
and franked by death, says:
*Never more, Daddy, never more.*
The waves roll over and strike
with the force and with the staggering
gesture of time's blindness.
Nostalgia sends us your beautiful
postcards from the dark.

# Infidelities

They were the small hours
when your footsteps still ring out
as they approach the door on to the street.
I'm telling you about my loneliness.
About my body waiting for you in the shadows,
the shadows of a room in a house
we'll never go back to, in the city
that's shining and icy now in the night
where, with my hands, I was sketching
the shape of your body on the sheet.
Until I heard your footsteps stopping,
the key entering the lock.
That key burned in the lock.
It was not a trivial thing. Nor is it now.
Deceit digs underground, it's a miner
filthy with coal-dust, with a glowing lamp on his head:
in this way it can cut across a whole life.

## Window

With the light off I gaze at the night.
The massive shadow of the cypress
can barely be made out. Uncertainty is here, and cold,
Venus shines at an angle
and everything is beginning to freeze, just as within me.
When a man grows old he often stands
stock still and gazes out at the night,
like someone who, before he travels there, studies
the street-map of an unknown city.

# Three women

A photograph taken
three years after war had ended.
It's the garden, in fact a neglected yard
that lay behind the house.
Not one of us there is smiling.
Fear steeps these garments, so often
torn and mended, as families are.
We're looking straight at the camera: my mother
with the swept-up hair-do of a film about
occupied France.
My grandmother twists a handkerchief in her hands
for one of her sons, still in prison.
I hardly remember the other woman:
weakened with so much suffering, my aunt
died of a heart attack a few months later.
Amidst the three of them, astride a bike,
four-years-old, grave-faced, I look like an adult.
How little there remains,
stored in memory's poky little room,
overlooking the dry garden of an autumn
with ghosts of roses: the garden
of childhood, fear's backyard.

# Ballad of the old merchant-ship

Under a sky of a dirty mauve colour,
I walk across the stones of the beach
where you swam for so many summers.
It's drizzling and there's an undertow. The bad weather
means that nobody from the village comes down to the sea.
The wind spatters me as though with tears.
The sea will help me to tell you a story.

There was once a merchant ship.
The hull's timbers shone, well-painted.
In the engine-room, with all the lights on,
the long steel shafts that turn the propellers
were greased and gleaming.
With the holds all full and cargo
stowed even up on deck,
it sailed across all the oceans.
Already, my stories are as desolate
as the stony beach from which I talk
to the girl who gazes at me from the waves.
Ships are always
a little like a toy,
but, as for the ship, its luck had changed:
imperceptible noises, shudderings,
slight faults and small parts,
fallen off, that no one replaced.
It began to stay
tied-up for weeks, and undertook
only tedious coastal trading.
The cargo it carried was cheap
and stank. No one ever
painted the hull, which grew rusty.
Often it would spring a leak.
I talk to you among the rocks of the beach
where you bathed for so many summers:
the waves and the stones keep up a murmuring
like a concrete-mixer. The horizon
is brightening as though you were going away
into the good weather: that's where the story
on the beach is ending.

The ship, listing, is on the high seas
with nobody on board: in the last storm
they all abandoned it.
Under a blue sky, on a calm sea,
the ship is starting to sink, little by little.

# Goodbye to Uncle Lluís

The war has not ended, it never ends,
and death is the Teruel front
where now the disastrous army is advancing
with the frost sparkling on their cloaks.
They are far off, a long way off, but they are already returning.

When he died he had only a handful of belongings,
among them a battered cassette with one tape.
I have listened to it: at first, for a long while
nothing could be heard but the rubbing of the machine.
Until suddenly, clear and melancholy,
there arose with force the song of a nightingale.
Leaving the cemetery I still hear
the lovely voice inside my head.
He will never go back to the river
to record the night-birds' singing.

# The dance of love

You're telling me what the last meeting was like.
I imagine the scene in that house of assignation:
the red light in the dark passage
and the wait behind a curtain.
*Don't ask any questions about what he took off,* you tell me.
Naked and feeling the cold floor under your feet,
you must have found the bathroom disgusting.

And what about him, what did he think? That you'd be upset
if the goodbye was in the usual flat?
*I didn't tell him.*
*In that bed with a mirror over it*
*he didn't know that that was goodbye.*
Sex has always made use of cunning:
in fact, you were already deceiving him with me.

A heartless time
because we were too young: we didn't know
that betrayal is a kind of love.
Later someone fell in love with me.
But when I tried to leave you,
you were the true love-affair,
because a loss can strike hard,
and be dazzling, sometimes. It was a glorious moment:
it's still bewildering to remember you
lying naked and desperate in my arms.
Sex is so despotic and so weak
that I fell in love with you all over again.

## Monument to the dead in the Korean War

*(Brooklyn)*

During my adolescent years
I collected those greyish cards
with photographs of soldiers,
American soldiers, who were my heroes.
Standing now in front of the list of the dead carved in stone,
I see my grandfather again, old and poor,
buying me the little envelopes: maybe some
of those soldiers in the photographs
are on this list. Growing old means putting
one's own brutal ending on every story.

# The dead

Those three blows from hands smacking the wall:
*Knock on the wall: who is going to fall?*
While they ring out we rush forward
then stop, watching Death whose back is turned,
but who will whirl round suddenly to catch out
anyone still teetering from their rush,
and eliminate them from that game forever.

*Knock on the wall: who is going to fall?*
The light is fading. Like a spot of gold, the candle
makes the shadows in the bedroom tremble.
Why is that postwar time so bitterly cold?
Death turns round and sees how my sister,
in her fever, tosses and cries under her ice-packs.

*Knock on the wall: who is going to fall?*
The past was my father's face:
prison-cells and scars, defections.
How the blows from those hands
smacking against the wall terrified him.
He cannot suppress a restless movement.
Anger and fear denounced him to Death.

*Knock on the wall: who is going to fall?*
We never strayed from its side.
And now I play with my dead child.
Why did I never read that look in her eyes?
But the future is crafty, and always cheats.
I never heard the three blows: she smiled at me
and her empty space was already beside me.
And the game had to go on.

*Knock on the wall: who is going to fall?*
I no longer care if Death can see me:
I turn round to smile at those who follow me.
Now that I've reached the wall,
I know nothing of what there might be behind it.
I only know I am going there with my dead.

# NOTES

**Self portrait** (28): At the end of the war, when times were hard, the warm cloaks worn by soldiers were used as extra bedding in many homes.

**The eyes in the rear-view mirror** (43): See note *(below)* about the collection *Joana* (91-114).

*Estació de França* (52-53): Lister was a famous, violent communist brigadier in the Spanish Civil War.

    *Santoña:* a large prison in the coastal town of Santander, on the north coast of Spain. During the final days of the war, the fugitive republican soldiers who had left the country by the eastern border, Catalonia, wanted to return to Spain from France by the western border, in the Basque Country. The nationalist army of Franco interned them in prison until some person with a solid (i.e. right-wing) reputation reclaimed them. The most famous prison for this "journey" was in Santoña.

**Uncle Lluís** (54): From the time of the Battle of the Ebro (spring 1938) the Spanish Civil War was already lost for the Republican Army.

**Piety** (57): The Mauser was a very common rifle in the Spanish Civil War.

**The suitcase** (58): The Rigat was a famous night-club of postwar Barcelona. It was in the Plaça de Catalunya.

**The German teacher** (64): 'After the Spanish Civil War, during my childhood under the fascist dictatorship, the Catalan language was forbidden, even though it was the mother tongue of most of people living in Catalonia. I was taught in Spanish in school. It was also the time of the end of the Second World War. This poem talks about those times.'

**Farewell** (65-67): *Indiano* is a man who after working many years in Spanish-American countries, goes back to live in Spain, in his native province, on private income.

    *guagua:* local name for a bus in the Canary Islands.

**Initiation** (68): In the time of Franco, the Spanish police wore a grey uniform, and the people called them 'the greys'.

**Paintings from an exhibition** (70-71): *joueurs de cartes*: card-players. *Hôtel de l'Avenir*: 'Hotel of the Future'.

**Dark night in Balmes Street** (74-75): See note *(below)* about the collection *Joana* (91-114).

**Sonnet in two cities** (77): A poem from the time of the fascist dictatorship. Margarit and his wife are young then, and they travel to Paris on a night train to buy the forbidden books, to see the forbidden films and to breathe the free air.

**Son in winter** (79): *Ciutat Vella:* in Catalan, Old City; the ancient district of Barcelona, near the Cathedral and the harbour.

**Joana** (91-114). Margarit's daughter, Joana, suffered from Rubinstein-Taybe syndrome, a mental condition which also involves severe physical problems, especially motor difficulties which compelled her to use crutches or a wheelchair. She understood that her well-being depended on the affection of those around her and she learned very early on that affection breeds more affection. But Margarit came to understand all this slowly and with difficulty, over a period of many years, and so 'Dark Night in Balmes Street', a poem set around the time of Joana's birth in 1970, reveals how badly prepared he was for this grief. The poem narrates and assesses facts he could not confront poetically (that is to say, in reality) until much later.

Thirty years after the night the poem discusses, the story came to a close with the last eight months of her life, which are the theme of the book, *Joana*. Her parents' anguish always led them to picture their daughter's defencelessness once they themselves had disappeared. As far as the poet is concerned, he does not know whether he is a better or worse person, but what he is convinced of is that, if he had not had Joana's constant company for those thirty years, he would be a lot worse. This is the theme of the poem, 'The eyes in the rear-view mirror', which celebrates his daughter's shining qualities.

**Fontana Metro** (96): *Gràcia* is a Barcelona district. Traditionally the home of people of modest means, it has today become fashionable, and in its narrow streets are a lot of bars, restaurants, little cinemas and shows. All have a certain romantic air thanks to the many young people of revolutionary, progressive, fringe and Catalan nationalist sympathies who patronise them.

**End** (101): The hill of Montjuïc, with Barcelona's cemetery, is a hill like a snout over the harbour in front the sea.

**Professor Bonaventura Bassegoda** (109): 'Bonaventura Bassegoda was a professor of Deep Foundations in the Architecture School of Barcelona. Those are the foundations of buildings going many metres into the ground.'

**Secrets** (123-24): Ramon de Campoamor was a popular late-romantic poet of the nineteenth century. 'The express train' is a long, famous love story about a train journey to Paris.

*Es Pujol* (125): *Es Pujol* ('The Hill') is a tiny street – a cul-de-sac – at the far end of Campanet, a little village in Mallorca.

**Entença Street** (130): The street in which the main prison of Barcelona stands.

**About my father and mother's honeymoon** (132): The military coup of 18 July 1936 by Franco against the Spanish Republic gave rise to the Spanish Civil War.

**Motorway** (133): When the Spanish Civil War began, Neruda was in Madrid with his first wife Maruca, a Dutch woman, and their hydrocephalic daughter, Malva Marina. Using war as a pretext, Neruda sent them to Holland and he stayed in Madrid with Delia del Carril, who was to be his second wife. He never saw them again. The child died eight years later and she was buried in the little cemetery of Gouda, in Holland.

**Landscape of La Conca** (135): Solivella and Blancafort are two small villages of central Catalonia. Near each one is a hill, and behind each hill a village: is not possible for them to see one another: the hills prevent it. But each village has its cemetery on top of its hill. Only the two cemeteries can look at one another.

**Structural calculations** (136): The city is Barcelona. The 'Diagonal' is a long avenue with, at one end, a university campus. At the end of the fifties, this area was still surrounded by fields.

**The sons of Captain Grant** (137). This poem takes its title from a famous Jules Verne novel. The Turó Park is a park of Barcelona.

**The dead** (167): This poem follows a children's game. There are similar versions of the game in a lot of countries. Facing a wall, a child smacks it three times with the palms of his hands and calls out the refrain of the game: this refrain in Catalonia is 'Un, dos, tres, pica paret' (*one, two, three, knock on the wall*). In the UK children would say *Knock on the wall: who is going to fall?* In the meantime, from a little way off, the rest of the children move forward. The child turns round, and, if someone is moving, he or she is out of the game.

171

# BIBLIOGRAPHY

## Works in Catalan

*Els primers freds: Poesia 1975-1995* (Col. Óssa Menor Sèrie Gran, Enciclopèdia Catalana, 2004). Collected edition comprising:
*Crònica* (1975)
*L'ordre del temps:poesia 1980-1984* (1984)
*Llum de pluja* (1986)
*Edat roja* (1991)
*Els motius del llop* (1993)
*Aiguaforts* (1995)
*Estació de França* (Hiperion, Madrid, 1999)
*Joana* (Col. Óssa Menor, Enciclopèdia Catalana, 2002)
*Càlcul d'estructures* (Col. Óssa Menor, Enciclopèdia Catalana, 2005)

## Individual anthologies in Catalan

*Remolcadors entre la boira* [poems about music] (Col. Veles i vents, L'Aixernador, 1995).
*Antologia del Navegant* (Maria de la Pau Cornadó, La Magrana, 1993)
*Poesia amorosa completa* (Col. Óssa Menor Sèrie Gran, Enciclopèdia Catalana, 2001)
*Trist el qui mai no ha perdut per amor una casa* (Col. Les eines, Enciclopèdia Catalana, 2001)

## Self-translation in Spanish

in bilingual editions (with the exception of *Edad roja*) :

*El primer frío: Poesía 1975-1995* (ed. Visor, Madrid, 2004). Collected edition comprising:
*Crónica* (1975)
*El orden del tiempo: poesía 1980-1984* (1984)
*Luz de lluvia* (1986)
*Edad roja* (1991) (translated by Antonio Jiménez Millán)
*Los motivos del lobo* (1993)
*Aguafuertes* (1995)
*Estación de Francia* (Hiperion, Madrid, 1999)
*Joana* (Hiperion, Madrid, 2002)
*Cálculo de estructuras* (Visor, Madrid, 2004)

## Individual anthologies in Spanish

*Cien poemas* [bilingual edition] (Col. La Veleta, ed. Comares. Granada, 1997)

*Luz de las obras* [bilingual edition; poems about architecture]. (Colegio de Arquitectos de Cádiz, 2000).

*Poesía amorosa completa* (Hiperion, Madrid, 2001) [exclusively in Spanish]

Antonio Jiménez Millán, *Amor y tiempo. La poesía de Joan Margarit* (Córdoba, ediciones Litopress, 2005)

*Arquitecturas de la memoria* [bilingual edition by José Luis Morante] (Madrid, Cátedra, col. Letras Hispánicas, 2006).

For full information on Joan Margarit's books and translations, go to www.joanmargarit.com